BEHIN⊔
THE SMALL
WOODEN DOOR

The Inside Story of
Parkhurst Prison

by
BRIAN MANSER

COACH HOUSE PUBLICATIONS LTD

Behind the small wooden door, the tiny, sparsely-equipped cell. Fixed to each cell door was an inscribed plate with the name of the prisoner, his number, his date of reception and the place of committal.

(Illustrated London News)

BEHIND THE SMALL WOODEN DOOR
The Inside Story of Parkhurst Prison

by Brian Manser

with the assistance of John Kingsbury

This book is dedicated to the memory of John Marriott

ISBN No. 1-899-392-181

Published by
Coach House Publications Ltd
The Coach House, School Green Road, Freshwater
Isle of Wight, PO40 9BB

Typeset by
K·F·Typography
Ward Road, Totland Bay, Isle of Wight, PO39 0BD

Printed by
The West Island Group Ltd
Afton Road, Freshwater, Isle of Wight, PO40 9TT

ACKNOWLEDGEMENTS

The realisation of this book owes much to the generous help received from the following individuals, institutions and organisations:

    Liz Black
    Jenny Brandis
    The Daily Mail
    Her Majesty's Prison Service
    The Historical Society of
        Ancient Buildings and Monuments
    Illustrated London News
    Isle of Wight County Press
    D. M. Morrison, Governor of Parkhurst Prison
    Western Australian Genealogical Society (Beverley Iffla)

There are, no doubt, others who we may have overlooked but no discourtesy is intended to anyone who has not been mentioned above. Our sincere thanks are extended to everyone who, by their help, enabled the Parkhurst Heritage Group to fulfil the ambition of publishing the history of Parkhurst Prison.

BRIAN MANSER
JOHN KINGSBURY

June 2000

CONTENTS

Foreword by Mr D. M. Morrison,
Governor of Parkhurst Prison   *xiii*

Preface   *xv*

Introduction   *xvii*

Queen Victoria's Charter
for the Establishment of Parkhurst Prison
– The Parkhurst Prison Act, 1838   *xxi*

Chapter 1   Wards, Work Routines and a Fire   1

Love Tokens   16

Chapter 2   Brief Early History and a Few Personalities   18

Chapter 3   Our Royal Visitor, the Women's Riots and
a Baby   27

Weapons and Gadgets   34

Chapter 4   More About the Doctor   37

Chapter 5   Through the Turn of the Century   44

Honouring Convict Heroes
– extract from the *IoW County Press*   51

Chapter 6   A Lull in the Excitement   55

Christmas Dinner, 1961   60

Chapter 7   Who Guards the Guards?   61

Chapter 8   The Next Three Decades   67

Escapes   74

Chapter 9   The Seventies and Eighties   79

One of the Lighter Moments   88

Chapter 10   To the End of the Twentieth Century
– Great Escapes   90

Appendix 1   Voyage of the *Simon Taylor*
             – the Australian connection   99

Appendix 2   The Story of John Gavin   101

Appendix 3   The Category System   113

Appendix 4   List of Governors and Deputy Governors
             – 1838 to the present day   115

FOREWORD

It is a pleasure to write this foreword for a book which is long overdue. Parkhurst is probably the prison name which everyone knows. Island residents and holiday-makers drive past and buy the Parkhurst mugs and T-shirts. It is very much a part of the Isle of Wight but few know much of its long and interesting history.

This book provides a fascinating record, told in a very human and informal way, about some of the highpoints in that history. It tells us about some of the bleak moments and of the harshness of bygone days; it tells of the humour which characterises all prisons but it also tells of the long tradition of care and humanity towards those we are charged with looking after.

Prisons are places of punishment but it is the prisoners' loss of liberty and not their treatment that is their punishment. Prisoners remain human beings with all the strengths and frailties of the rest of us. Our work is to try and change their criminal behaviour but our duty is to treat them with humanity whilst in custody.

Parkhurst has a very long and deserved reputation for its humanity and it is for that reason that I have been so proud to govern it. I am glad that the public can now know a little more of our past.

D. M. MORRISON
Governor

The original juvenile workshops are still standing. Until this year, the Parkhurst Heritage Group's collection of artefacts and prison memorabilia was temporarily housed in these buildings.

PREFACE

THE PARKHURST HERITAGE GROUP

The Parkhurst Heritage Group was the original idea of Principal Officer John Kingsbury who, with the permission of the then Governor, John Marriott, advertised for any staff at the prison who were interested in the history of the establishment to attend a meeting in John's office. I remember that the room was quite full with many interested parties. However, through no-one's fault, the group took a while to get started. Unfortunately, this resulted in some of the members dropping out through lack of interest, leaving behind a hard core of five dedicated officers.

We needed to raise funds so it was decided to hire a stand at the Isle of Wight Garlic Festival, held over the weekend of 20th-21st August 1994, where, for the very first time, we told the secrets of the establishment to the general public. The response was over-whelming. The four of us who took part were astonished at the level of interest from the, literally, hoards of people who constantly surrounded our tables, without a break, on both of the days we were there.

Before we went to the Festival, we had the foresight to buy a quantity of those 'tacky' souvenirs that are sold to the holiday-makers – the mugs that were 'stolen from Parkhurst', tea towels, key rings, baseball caps, and even sticks of rock with the legend 'Parkhurst' written right through them. Incredibly, we sold every-thing we could carry in the two days we were there. The group had proved that there is a curiosity about the prison from the general public. That made us even more determined to set the group up properly and try to achieve our main aim, which was to set up a museum for the artefacts that we were fast collecting from all around the prison.

We were just getting it nicely off the ground, when the 'Great Escape' occurred in 1995 and, of course, there were more impor-tant things to be occupied with. The same five officers were still there, but it was very hard to keep the interest going, especially as the prison was going through such a major upheaval. Eventually, after a period of two years, the prison finally settled down into its new rôle and it was decided to try to resurrect the Heritage Group. Due to staff postings and a host of other reasons only two of the original members remain today: myself – Brian Manser – and John Kingsbury. There are others who help out with some of our presentations, which last year (1999) included over forty talks to various groups Island-wide.

We have now partly achieved one of our original objectives – we have a museum within the walls of the prison, which is large enough to house our growing collection of documents and arte-facts, some of which have been donated by complete strangers. In the future we plan to build on these achievements. There is an urgent need to recruit more like-minded officers who are willing to give up their own time to help pass on the fascinating story of this penal establishment to the people who live on the outside of its walls.

INTRODUCTION

WHERE AND WHY

Her Majesty's Prison, Parkhurst is situated in the centre of the Isle of Wight, about two miles north of Newport, the Island's capital. In close proximity are the prisons of Albany and Camphill, which together form nearly one square mile of penal establishments, making it one of the largest complexes in Europe.

Parkhurst has been in existence for over 160 years and during that period of time has quietly gone about the normal day-to-day running of what amounts to a small village. However, there have been times when Parkhurst has been the centre of the world's media attention, usually for the wrong reasons.

The local population, and indeed the holiday-makers, who pass by its walls on a regular basis cannot have much idea of what goes on inside. It is therefore the intention of this book to let out a few of our secrets, to inform, entertain and amuse the reader. There is no intention of glorifying the regime inside the establishment, which, at times, bordered on the barbaric, the frightening and, occasionally, even the hilarious. This is just a simple attempt to tell it as it is.

If the foregoing provides us, very briefly, with a summary of the location and longevity of Parkhurst then, to further set the scene, the following extract from the Governor's Journal, Pentonville Prison, November 1842, gives us an indication of the reason behind its existence:

"My wish is, that Pentonville will be for adults what Parkhurst is for Juvenile Offenders: a prison of instructions and probation rather than a gaol of oppressive punishment; excepting that the more severe discipline of the separate system in Pentonville is applied to those of riper years, while the tender youth of Parkhurst is not exposed to the full rigor of this salutary discipline."

The views that are expressed in this book are those of the Parkhurst Heritage Group and do not necessarily reflect those of the Prison Service.

The Pump House. This small brick block was originally constructed in 1847, fitted with hand cranks which the inmates turned to draw water from the well inside. After Parkhurst was connected to the mains water supply, the building was used as the prison synagogue until 1937 and as the prison boardroom from then to 1996. It remained empty until March 2000 when conversion work began to create a permanent Heritage Centre for the display of the Parkhurst Heritage Group's collection. A replica of an original cell has been built as a feature of the exhibits.

A view of Parkhurst Prison in Victorian times, seen from the Cowes to Newport Road.

The interior of the court seen from the gateway, with the Governor's House and the Steward's Office in the centre. They were formerly part of the hospital barracks.

(Illustrated London News)

THE PARKHURST PRISON ACT 1838

This is a copy of the Act of Parliament that set up Parkhurst as the first prison aimed at the reformation of young offenders. In its first years it was severely criticised for the strictness of its regime which included the use of leg irons and severe punishment. In later years under the governorship of Captain George Hall it achieved considerable success. A change of government policy in the late 1850's interfered with his methods and the prison ceased to be a young offender prison in 1863.

C A P. LXXXII.

An Act for establishing a Prison for young Offenders.   [10th *August* 1838.]

‘ **W**HEREAS it may be of great public Advantage that a Prison be provided in which
‘ young Offenders may be detained and corrected, and may receive such Instruction
‘ and be subject to such Discipline as shall appear most conducive to their Reformation and
‘ to the Repression of Crime: And whereas the Buildings at *Parkhurst* in the *Isle of Wight*,
‘ lately used as a Military Hospital and as a Medical Asylum for the Children of Soldiers,
‘ are Buildings which may be conveniently used for such a Prison ;’ be it therefore enacted
by the Queen's most Excellent Majesty, by and with the Advice and Consent of the Lords
Spiritual and Temporal, and Commons, in this present Parliament assembled, and by the
Authority of the same, That it shall be lawful for Her Majesty, by Warrant under the Royal
Sign Manual, to appoint that the said Buildings at *Parkhurst* shall be used as a Prison for
the Confinement of such Offenders as are herein-after specified, as soon as the same can be
fitted and completed for that Purpose; and the said Buildings shall thereupon become a Prison
for the lawful Confinement of such Offenders, and shall be within the Provisions of an Act
passed in the Sixth Year of the Reign of His late Majesty, intituled *An Act for effecting
greater Uniformity of Practice in the Government of the several Prisons in England and Wales,
and for appointing Inspectors of Prisons in* Great Britain. *(margin: Her Majesty may appoint the Buildings at Parkhurst to be used as a Prison for juvenile Offenders. 5 & 6 W. 4. c. 38.)*

II. And be it enacted, That it shall be lawful for One of Her Majesty's Principal Secretaries
of State to appoint for *Parkhurst* Prison a Governor, a Chaplain being a Clergyman not having
any other Cure of Souls, a Surgeon, a Matron, and such other Officers, Assistants, and
Servants as may be necessary for the Service and Discipline of the Prison, and at Pleasure to
remove all or any of the said Governor, Chaplain, Surgeon, Matron, and other Officers,
Assistants, and Servants, and to appoint others in their Room, and to fix the Salaries to be
paid to each of them. *(margin: Officers to be appointed by the Crown.)*

III. And be it enacted, That it shall be lawful for One of Her Majesty's Principal Secre-
taries of State to direct the Removal to *Parkhurst* Prison of any young Offender, Male or
Female, as well those under Sentence or Order of Transportation as those under Sentence of
Imprison- *(margin: Young Offenders under Sentence may be removed to Parkhurst Prison.)*

The Parkhurst Prison Act of 1838.

Imprisonment, who, having been examined by an experienced Surgeon or Apothecary, shall appear to be free from any putrid or infectious Distemper, and fit to be removed from the Gaol, Prison, or Place in which such Offender shall be confined : Provided always, that every Offender so removed, who shall be under Sentence of Transportation, shall nevertheless be within the Provisions of an Act passed in the Fifth Year of the Reign of King *George* the

5 G. 4. c. 84.

Fourth, intituled *An Act for the Transportation of Offenders from* Great Britain, in case the Secretary of State shall direct that he or she shall be afterwards removed from *Parkhurst* Prison as herein-after provided.

Term of Imprisonment in Parkhurst Prison.

IV. And be it enacted, That every Offender who shall be so removed to *Parkhurst* Prison shall continue there until he or she shall be transported according to Law, or shall become entitled to his or her Liberty, or until the Secretary of State shall direct the Removal of such Offender to the Gaol, Prison, or Place from which he or she shall have been brought, or in

Gaolers, &c. having the Custody of Offenders ordered to be placed there shall cause them to be delivered to the Governor thereof.

which he or she may be lawfully confined ; and the Sheriff, Gaoler, or other Person having the Custody of any Offender whose Removal to *Parkhurst* Prison shall be ordered in manner aforesaid shall, with all convenient Speed after the Receipt of any such Order, convey or cause to be conveyed every such Offender to *Parkhurst* Prison, and shall there deliver him or her to the Governor of the Prison, with a true Copy, attested by such Sheriff or Gaoler, of the Caption and Order of the Court by which such Offender was sentenced, containing the Sentence of every such Offender by virtue whereof he or she shall be in the Custody of such Sheriff or Gaoler, and also a Certificate specifying such Particulars within the Knowledge of the Sheriff or Gaoler concerning such Offender as may be from Time to Time directed by the Secretary of State; and the Governor shall give a Receipt in Writing to the Sheriff or Gaoler for his Discharge; and all reasonable Expences which the Sheriff or Gaoler shall incur in every such Removal shall be paid by the County, Riding, Division, City, Borough, Liberty, or Place for which the Court in which the Offender was convicted shall have been holden.

As to Offenders removed from Parkhurst Prison as incorrigible.

V. And be it enacted, That it shall be lawful for the Secretary of State at any Time to order any Offender to be removed from *Parkhurst* Prison as incorrigible, and in every such Case the Offender so removed shall be liable to be transported or confined, under his or her original Sentence or Sentences of Transportation or Imprisonment, to the full Extent of the Term or Terms specified in such Sentence or Sentences, and shall be subject to all the Consequences of such Sentence or Sentences, in the same Manner as if no Order for sending him or her to *Parkhurst* Prison had been made.

Powers of the Governor.

VI. And be it enacted, That after the Delivery of any such Offender as aforesaid into the Custody to which he or she shall be so ordered as aforesaid, such Governor or other Person having the Custody of Offenders under his Direction shall, during the Term for which such Offender shall remain in his Custody, have the same Powers over such Offender as are incident to the Office of a Sheriff or Gaoler, and in case of any Abuse of such Custody, or other Misbehaviour or Negligence in the Discharge of his Office, shall be liable to the same Punishment as a Gaoler is now liable to by Law.

Secretary of State to make Regulations for the Government of the Prison.

VII. And be it enacted, That the Secretary of State shall be empowered from Time to Time to make Rules for the Government and Regulation of *Parkhurst* Prison, and for the Discipline of the Offenders imprisoned therein, and to subscribe a Certificate that they are fit to be enforced ; and all such Rules shall be laid before Parliament within Six Weeks after such Rules shall be certified, or if Parliament be not then sitting, within Six Weeks after the next Meeting of Parliament.

Corporal Punishment may be inflicted in Parkhurst Prison.

VIII. And be it enacted, That it shall be lawful for the Secretary of State from Time to Time to specify, by such Regulations as aforesaid, such Offences which, if committed in *Parkhurst* Prison by Male Convicts, shall appear to him deserving of corporal Punishment ; and if any Male Offender in *Parkhurst* Prison shall commit any Offence whereby he shall under any Regulation then in force become liable to corporal Punishment, the Governor of the said Prison shall have Power to inflict such Punishment.

Visitors to be appointed by the Queen in Council.

IX. And be it enacted, That as soon as the said Buildings shall be appointed to be used as a Prison as aforesaid for the Reception of Offenders it shall be lawful for Her

8   Majesty,

Majesty, with the Advice of Her Privy Council, to nominate and appoint Three or more fit and discreet Persons to be Visitors of the said Prison, and from Time to Time to remove all or any of such Visitors and appoint others in their Stead, or in the Stead of such as shall die or resign or be unable by Sickness or otherwise to attend; and One or more of such Visitors shall personally visit such Prison at least Three Times in each Quarter of a Year, and oftener if Occasion shall require, and shall examine into the Behaviour and Conduct of the respective Officers, and the Treatment, Behaviour, and Condition of the Prisoners, and of all Abuses within the Prison, and if he or they shall discover any Abuse or Abuses therein he or they is or are hereby required to report the same in Writing to One of Her Majesty's Principal Secretaries of State.

X. And be it enacted, That the said Visitors shall make a half-yearly Report in Writing to One of Her Majesty's Principal Secretaries of State concerning the State and Condition of such Prison, and of any Abuse or Abuses which they may have observed or have reason to believe to exist in the said Prison or in the Management of the Prison, as well as of the general State of the Prisoners as to Morals, Discipline, and Employment, and Observance of Rules. *(marginal note: Visitors to report the State of the Prison to the Secretary of State.)*

XI. ' And whereas Her Majesty has lately exercised Her Royal Prerogative of Mercy ' in granting Pardons to young Offenders who have been sentenced to Transportation or ' Imprisonment, upon the Condition of placing himself or herself under the Care of some ' charitable Institution for the Reception and Reformation of young Offenders named in ' such Pardon, and conforming to and abiding by the Orders and Rules thereof: And ' whereas the same has been found beneficial: And whereas it is expedient that some ' Provision should be made for carrying the same more fully into effect;' be it therefore further enacted, That from and after the passing of this Act, in case any young Offender who has been or shall be hereafter sentenced to Transportation or Imprisonment has been or shall be pardoned by Her Majesty for such Offence upon such Condition as aforesaid, and has or shall accept such conditional Pardon, and shall afterwards abscond from such Institution, or wilfully neglect or refuse to abide by and conform to the Rules thereof, it shall and may be lawful to and for any Justice of the Peace acting in and for the County, City, Riding, or Division wherein the said Offender shall actually be at the Time he shall so abscond or neglect or refuse as aforesaid, upon due Proof thereof made before him upon the Oath of One credible Witness, by Warrant under his Hand and Seal to commit the Party so offending for every such Offence to any Gaol or House of Correction for the said County, City, Riding, or Division, with or without hard Labour, for any Period not exceeding Three Calendar Months for the First Offence and not exceeding Six Calendar Months for the Second or any subsequent Offence, in case the Managers or Directors of any such charitable Institution shall be willing to receive any such young Offender after his or her being convicted of absconding, neglecting, or refusing as aforesaid; and in every Case such Imprisonment shall be in addition to the original Sentence of such young Offender; and after the Expiration of the Time of such additional Punishment, if the Managers or Directors of any such charitable Institution shall refuse to receive such Offender, or if Her Majesty shall not be pleased to exercise Her Royal Prerogative in pardoning the Breach of the Condition on which the former Pardon was granted, the said Party shall forfeit all Benefit of the said Pardon, and shall be remitted to the original Sentence, and shall undergo the Residue thereof, as if no such Pardon had been granted. *(marginal note: Offenders pardoned conditionally may be committed to House of Correction if they break the Condition, or remitted to their former Sentence.)*

XII. And be it enacted, That if any Offender who shall be ordered to be confined in Parkhurst Prison shall at any Time during the Term of such Confinement break Prison or escape from the Place of his or her Confinement, or in his or her Conveyance to such Place of Confinement, or from any Lands belonging to the Prison, or from the Person or Persons having the lawful Custody of such Offender, he or she so breaking Prison or escaping shall be punished, if under Sentence of Imprisonment, by an Addition not exceeding Two Years to the Term for which he or she at the Time of his or her Breach of Prison or Escape was subject to be confined, and if under Sentence of Transportation, in such Manner as Persons under Sentence of Transportation escaping from or breaking out of any other Prison or Place of Confinement are liable to be punished; and if an Offender so punished by such *(marginal note: Offenders breaking Prison, &c.)*

CHAPTER ONE

Wards, Work Routines and a Fire

U P TO the mid-nineteenth century, children as young as six or seven who had been convicted of and sentenced for a crime would have had to serve their time in adult prisons. What was even worse for these young children is that they were sent, on a regular basis, to serve their sentence on board one of the rotting hulks that were anchored offshore, around the coast. These youngsters were locked up in appalling conditions, often with older and much hardened criminals. It goes without saying that these poor and unfortunate children were wide open to corruption and abuse by both jailers and fellow convicts.

It was the first Duke of Wellington who raised the question in the House of Lords concerning the urgent need to build a special prison to house young children. They could then be protected from the depraved and often vicious environment of the adult prisons.

In 1834 an all-party Select Committee was appointed to try to identify an alternative to keeping young children on the hulks. The committee suggested a shore-based prison to be either built or converted from existing buildings somewhere with easy access to the sea for transportation. It was also proposed that, in order to save money, an old military barracks could be converted into a prison. Albany Barracks – a large army training camp – was put forward as a possible location, but this was rejected in favour of the old military hospital at Parkhurst. The Bill to build the prison was passed in 1838 and signed by Queen Victoria.

One of the earliest inmates to be received into Parkhurst was twelve-year old Nathaniel Barton who was not by any means a hardened criminal like many others of his peer group. He was just a very immature young man who mistakenly believed that the revenge he sought against his master could satisfy his anger whilst not denying him of his freedom and liberty.

Nathaniel was born in 1830 in a small hamlet called Tendron, near Colchester in Essex. His father, Joseph, was a farm labourer who earned ten shillings (fifty pence) a week. His mother made herself busy around the house, occasionally taking in washing, or helping out in the fields at harvest time to raise a few extra pennies for the housekeeping. When he was young, Nathaniel attended a local charity school for nearly a year where he was taught the basics of reading and writing. Being a quick learner, he soon picked up a good skill level in these important subjects. After school he would work with his father in the fields, helping out with the crops or attending to the small herd of cattle belonging to his master, his favourite task. One day he was very severely reprimanded by his employer for allowing the cattle to escape their compound and damage some nearby crops. Nathaniel deeply resented this rebuke and he resolved to gain revenge for the telling off he received.

A few days later, along with two of his friends, William Saxby, aged nine, and Henry Smith, aged just eight, they stole some lucifers (matches) from a nearby cottage and set fire to some straw stacks. Started just after dinner, the fire was quickly spotted by Nathaniel's father who raced across to the scene and made a gallant but futile attempt to extinguish the flames. The master immediately suspected the young lad and charged him and his two young accomplices with the crime. All three readily confessed to the arson and, at a later date, pleaded guilty at the Chelmsford Assizes.

The punishment imposed on the boys, for what was after all no more than a misdemeanour, must have come as an awful shock, especially to the youngest, Henry, who at eight years old was sentenced, the same as the other two, to fifteen years Transportation to the Colonies. They were sentenced on the 15th July 1844 and the sorry trio were immediately removed from the Assizes to the infamous Millbank Prison, on the north bank of the Thames. There, they were to await their eventual transfer to Parkhurst.

If the shock of the very heavy sentence, and the upheaval of being removed from a safe family environment to the harsh realities of a primitive Victorian gaol, was not enough, yet another, far-reaching blow lay in store for them. The law of the land at that time stated that no child under the age of fourteen should be transported. Young Henry Smith, at eight years of age, was the youngest of the trio and well below the minimum age required by law. Therefore, Henry would be incarcerated at Parkhurst, until the age of fourteen, when he would then be sent to the Colonies to start his fifteen years sentence. In effect, this meant that he was going to serve twenty-one years and not the original fifteen he had been sentenced to. If he were not already remorseful, as the chain of events unfolded, the realisation of the extent of his punishment would surely have made him so!

In fact, there is a reasonably happy ending to the sad tale of poor Henry. The transportation order was rescinded, so he did not have to go to Australia. Instead, he was allowed to serve his time, in this country, at a philanthropic institution. These charitable institutions were set up by the Victorians to take in homeless waifs and strays, to protect them from the dangers of the streets.

In September of the same year, Nathaniel and seventeen other boy convicts arrived at Parkhurst, having spent the best part of two days travelling from London. An overnight stop was arranged for the party at the Royal Anchor public house, in Liphook, Hampshire. On arrival there, late at night, the young inmates were given a hot meal of beef stew, potatoes, and bread. They were then divided into two groups, one of which spent the night chained to the wall, in a room adjacent to the keg store, in the cellar. The remaining nine inmates were chained to some secure 'O' rings, mounted to a strong part of the garret of the building. Sleep did not come easy for them that night. Apart from the hard floorboards and primitive sleeping arrangements, the noise of the prison warders drinking kept them awake until the early hours of the morning. Time to reflect, possibly, on what lay ahead of them at Parkhurst, and later, in the Colonies.

In a lot of ways, young offenders in Queen Victoria's time were far better off in prison than many of the children of the same age who still enjoyed their freedom on the streets. This was resented by many, for, after all, the young criminal had the benefit of proper warm clothing, good boots, food and accommodation, and an education, all of which was denied to and, no doubt, envied by the children who fought a daily survival battle on the streets. It was a matter, too, which attracted the attention of some very prominent people.

3

Mary Carpenter was a social reformer of that era though with very different aspirations compared with her modern equivalent. She was also quite a popular, famous and influential person of the day. She campaigned endlessly against prison regimes, saying that the treatment given to these young offenders was far too good for them and did not act as a deterrent to discourage them from re-offending. Parkhurst was even dubbed as an academy for young gentlemen by the popular press. However, it pleases me to report that Parkhurst weathered that particular storm, as indeed it has done many others since.

So, although the conditions inside the walls of Parkhurst were reasonably comfortable, the regime was very disciplined, which was something that took a lot of getting used to by some of the inmates. Based on Military Training, the strict rules and regulations were designed to bring these young lawbreakers back to the way that society wished them to be – good, hard working and God-fearing. Should one of the many and, in a lot of cases, trivial rules be broken, the young inmate could expect the full weight of the discipline code to come crashing down on him. There are many instances in the prison journals of very minor misdemeanours, certainly when measured by modern day standards, being punished with such ferocity that today it would be looked upon as sheer brutality.

Nathaniel Barton remained at Parkhurst just two days short of four years. The surviving journals show that he broke the rules and was punished on five occasions. Most of his punishments were awarded for repeated misconduct, either in the school, or whilst working on the land. His worst punishment was to be confined for three days, for wantonly damaging his boots and then lying about it. For boys who persistently played up, the authorities had a couple of particularly nasty forms of punishment that were administered with alarming regularity. They could have been whipped or put into the much-feared 'Black Hole'. The administration of either of these punishments should have been enough to deter any inmate from wanting to receive them again. Sadly, though, there are many instances of these practices being inflicted again and again on the same individual with apparently no deterrent value whatsoever.

Use of the whip is self-explanatory. Commonly, twenty lashes were awarded to the poor unfortunate who was always flogged publicly, the other inmates ordered to stand and watch the proceedings, presumably as a deterrent to them. The crimes that warranted such a punishment were varied. One of the commonest reasons was for creating a disturbance in either the school or, more often, in the dormitories. The use of foul language or the wanton destruction of either uniform or equipment were also high on the whipping list.

The 'Black Hole' requires a little explanation. Adjacent to the building known today as 'C' Wing, there is a flight of twelve steps, which lead down to the cellars. In Nathaniel Barton's time, these cellars would have housed the bathhouse, the boiler room, and the punishment cells known as the 'Black Hole'. It consists of an underground brick-built cell with a curved roof, divided into two by a wall. The whole structure was designed to house very disruptive prisoners in the short term. A small wooden door led into the cell, the area of which was no more than nine feet by four feet. The only 'fittings' in the cell were a small grill that would allow fresh air to circulate and a hole in the floor that led directly into the sewer, used for all sanitation requirements. As a form of punishment, the young prisoners would be placed in this cell, sometimes in restraints, for periods of up to three days. Needless to say there would be no natural light at all, hence its nickname.

Generally, three to six hours seems to have been the average time for meting out this form of punishment on the boys, although we do have a record of one young man who, in a period of seven nights, spent six of them alone, in darkness, in the cellars. This particularly scary form of punishment was awarded for all sorts of misdemeanours. Sixteen-year-old John Taylor was handcuffed and whipped 36 times as a punishment for his previous bad behaviour. After being placed back into his cell by the warders, he became riotous, and was then removed to the 'Black Hole' where he stayed for the next three days, presumably to calm down after the whipping. A year later, and young John was unfortunately placed back in the 'Hole' for his second visit. This time the boy had managed to break out of his cell, striking and kicking Assistant Warder Meaden who caught and restrained him. For this assault on the staff, Taylor spent 48 hours in the 'Hole'. During the first 15 hours of his ordeal, he was placed in irons. In yet another extreme case, James Berry and Joseph Hooper, both fourteen years of age, were given 36 and 48 hours respectively, simply for bed-wetting. Whether this rather bizarre cure ended their bed-wetting problem is unfortunately not recorded. Somehow I doubt it!

A less hurtful or scary form of punishment was used to correct those inmates who persistently 'stepped over the line'. These boys would be back-staged for periods of up to a month to the Miscon-duct Class. This class was completely detached from the normal regime and the boys in it could expect a much harsher code of discipline for the duration. Extra drill, more in-cell work, generally oakum picking, and virtually no free time to themselves, were all they could look forward to until they had served their punishment and were 'promoted' back to the normal Halls.

Reading through the Governor's Journal of 1844, reveals some very severe punishments for quite petty offences, certainly when judged by modern day standards. It must be remembered, however, that, in Victorian society, young men could expect to be dealt with by the authorities with extreme severity. There are cases of children sentenced to transportation simply for stealing a pair of stockings. What is not clear, in these cases, is whether these were the first offences to be committed or the last in a long line of petty law-breaking. Broken rules, either inside or outside of the prison walls, were not tolerated. Judge for yourself from these examples taken from some of Parkhurst's journals:

James Bennet was awarded 24 hours in the 'Black Hole' for refusing to have his hair cut.

George Carley, whipped 36 times for causing a disturbance in the dining hall.

John Martin, confined to his cell for 24 hours because he failed to complete the knitting he was issued to do.

Bartholomew Shearn was whipped 22 times for whistling in his dormitory. On reading this I can only assume that young Bart was whistling in a violent manner!

Finally, a word or two about one fifteen-year-old boy, whose stay at Parkhurst was not a very happy one. James Cleland, an orphan, was convicted in 1845 of housebreaking and was subsequently sentenced to seven years transportation. He arrived at Parkhurst on 11th April of that year, remaining there for a total of four years and five months. During this period young James collected no fewer than 46 disciplined entries against him in the journal. So many, in fact, that the recording officer had to paste a spare page in the book to accommodate all the extra entries. Altogether, this young man spent 67 days confined to his cell, he was whipped on three separate occasions and made a total of four trips to the 'Black Hole'.

I do confess to having a little sympathy for Master Cleland for having to endure all this punishment for what was, for the most part, very petty rule breaking. We can assume that, to allow himself to be constantly punished in the way that he was, James Cleland was probably mentally unbalanced. On one occasion James was whipped 36 strokes for tearing his blanket, and cutting his hand in the process. He was frog-marched to the 'Black Hole',

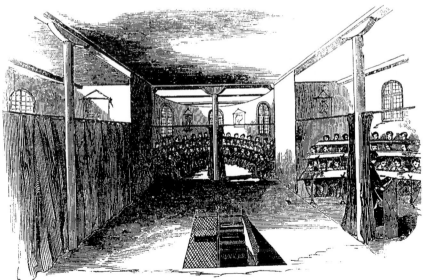

The General Ward school room, divided into two main sections, each further sub-divided.

(Illustrated London News)

7

where he was kept for a few hours, to calm down. I dare say that it could be argued that if James was not mentally unbalanced when he went to Parkhurst, by the time he left he might well have been. He sailed to Van Diemans Land (now Tasmania) on 3rd August 1849, on the ship *Adelaide*. I do hope somebody had the foresight to warn Australia that he was coming.

A total of 4,088 boys passed through Parkhurst's gates. Not all of them were transported. Many were released to charitable organizations in England where they would have been brought up in a more appropriate environment. Many others were pardoned and released back into the protection of their family. Sadly, one young man never left the prison for he was unfortunately run over and killed by a loaded handcart.

Parkhurst was divided into two main areas, the Upper and Lower Prisons. The Upper Prison would accommodate boys from the age of fifteen upwards. The Lower Prison housed boys as young as six or seven years old through to the age of fifteen.

The Probationary Ward school room. On first arrival, the boy prisoners were received in the Probationary Ward which was divided down the middle by the Corridor. On either side were three tiers of cells, 137 in total.

(Illustrated London News)

The Corridor was equipped with apparatus for raising food to the galleries, styled on similar equipment at Pentonville Prison. The prisoners in the Probationary Ward ate their meals in their cells.

(Illustrated London News)

The Probationary Ward was situated in the Lower Prison and it was to here that all new receptions would go for the first few months of their sentence. The accommodation block here was locally known as the 'corridor', which was a large three tier structure, consisting of 137 brick arched cells each measuring 11 feet by 7 feet. All of the cells were provided with the most basic of facilities. A small table, stool and writing desk, were the only items of furniture issued. The inmates were also allowed to have a Bible,

During lessons or services, the prisoners were unable to see each other, only the Chaplain or teacher.

prayer and hymn books and, for schooling purposes, a slate and pencil. Each prisoner was also issued with a rolled up hammock, which was suspended from specially fitted cleats, fifteen inches above the ground. In this Ward, all meals were eaten in the cells, from which the boys were allowed to be absent for only six hours a day. The time outside of the cell comprised ninety minutes exercise, two and a half hours of schooling (alternate days only!), thirty minutes for morning cleaning, and the same period in the evening for prayers. Boys were held on this Ward for an average of five months depending on their individual behaviour.

The Probationary Ward inmates were always segregated from each other and the rest of the prison regime, even to the extent of shielding the boys with large wooden partitions during Chapel services. Such education they received was given in the two school periods allocated on alternate mornings. The subjects varied but tended to lean towards religious and moralistic subjects. All schooling was conducted, like the religious services, with the pupils sitting in fifty or so specially constructed wooden compartments that were built in such a manner that the school-master could see all of his charges perfectly well, but they could neither see, nor converse with each other!

By obtaining good marks for both knowledge and behaviour, the boys would qualify for the next higher structure of schooling, which was the General Wards. Here they were taught the same subjects as before, but with the addition of arithmetic, writing and general geography but although the school hours were increased to five hours, tuition still took place on alternate days. Other periods were taken up with activities such as labour, which took the form of shoe-making, carpentry, brick-making or the general maintenance of the various structures within the prison walls. Outside the gate there was a flourishing market garden, which helped to offset the running costs of the establishment by supplying a lot of its own fruit and vegetables. Drill was not a popular subject with the boys. It is not surprising really as it seems that most of the staff came from military backgrounds and used drill to instil a sense of discipline into the inmates, to get them used to accepting orders without question.

It goes without saying that the accommodation areas must

The Shoemakers' Department.
(Illustrated London News)

have shone like the proverbial new pin, judging by the amount of cleaning activities that went on. Even whilst locked up, the inmates were set work to do. Oakum picking was one of the more typical tasks that had to be done. Old pieces of tarred rope were first weighed and then given to the inmates for them to split down into individual fibres. This material was then used for a variety of purposes, most commonly for caulking the wooden decks of ships to seal the joints between the timbers. The reason why the material was weighed in its raw state was because some of the boys tried to cut corners. Very simply they would hide some of the material in the air grill in their cell, to save them effort and hopefully dupe the warder into believing that they had completed the task. Unfortunately, by the time they realised that the warder carried scales, it was too late and they were punished quite severely for their devious tactics.

It is also recorded that the inmates were taught how to knit, although by whom is not known. After they had grasped the basics, they were given rough wool, called 'worsted', a pair of wooden knitting needles, and then instructed what to make. It is a shame that the surviving journals do not record the finished products.

Another task worthy of mention, was that of the pump party. Still located in the prison today is the original well that at one time supplied all of the water needed for the day-to-day running of the establishment. This well is rumoured to be over 270 feet deep. In recent years a camera was lowered down it but unfortunately it could not get deeper than 82 feet because of all the old iron ladders that were once fixed to the side which have corroded away and fallen to the bottom over the years.

Each day a small party of boys would have been marched to the pump-house, remaining there lifting water until the day's quota was stored above ground. Bath-days were probably the busiest. There is no record of water being stored anywhere in the event of a fire, although it probably was. It would certainly have been needed on the evening of 3rd August 1850.

Shortly after midnight, the watchman from the Lower Prison discovered that one of the dormitories was on fire. The alarm was raised, and the first to respond were the soldiers from the nearby Albany Barracks, who arrived with their engine. The soldiers formed long lines for the purpose of passing buckets of water hand to hand. Minutes later two engines from the House of Industry (the polite name for the Workhouse, which is now part of the old St Mary's Hospital) arrived, under the supervision of the Governor, Mr Clark, who also brought with him several able bodied paupers to provide assistance. Just after one o'clock in the morning two more engines arrived from Newport, but it was too late to save the building, so all efforts were now directed instead at saving the surrounding structures, especially the stores.

As soon as the alarm had been sounded, the juveniles were rescued, and every effort was taken to ensure their safe custody. However, the fire took hold with such speed that it was necessary to order the boys to break out of their cells, which they did. If that order had not been promptly given, then it is a certainty that lives would have been lost. All the inmates were quickly accounted for, some in a state of complete nakedness. Once this had been completed, all the prisoners were marched onto the parade ground where they sat and watched the proceedings unfold, guarded by a handful of soldiers. The fire had originated in the Dormitory on 'C' Ward, a large building some 200 feet long by 25 feet wide. Brick built, of three storeys, all of its interior fittings were solidly constructed of wood. On the night of the fire there were two hundred prisoners in the Ward.

Eventually, by about 4 a.m., the fire was brought under control, after the roof of the building had collapsed into itself, leaving the external walls and chimney stacks free standing. Such was the heat of the interior that 200 iron bedsteads had melted into unrecognisable lumps of scrap metal. The source of the fire was later discovered to have been in one of the chimney flues.

Apart from Major Alves, who commanded the Albany Garrison, the only other person to be mentioned in the press reports at the time of the fire was Mr George Shirlaw, who was the Deputy-Governor of the prison. It is reported that during the fire, his exertions were most humane and indefatigable, with regard to ensuring the well-being of his inmates.

Mr Shirlaw had been a Battalion Sergeant Major in the Royal Artillery before joining the Prison service and because of his previous rank he was promoted to Chief Officer. However, due to the long absences of the Governor on prison business, and through illness, the Home Office appointed Shirlaw as the first Deputy-Governor, not only at Parkhurst, but in the entire Prison Service. He quickly proved to be an excellent manager, using his military experience to good effect on a number of instances, one of which will be described later in the book.

To return to the story of Nathaniel Barton, at the age of fifteen he was moved into the Upper Prison where he did not take long to adjust to his new surroundings. This relocation was only temporary, however, for a few weeks later he, together with several of his peers, was taken to a ship moored in the Solent by the name of the *Eden*. This ship set sail on 26th September 1848, fully laden with over 250 convicts destined for Port Phillip, Western Australia. As far as we know, Nathaniel never again set foot on English soil but he left behind a permanent reminder of himself in the form of a love token that he sent to his mother a few weeks before he sailed. He had managed to lay his hands on an old copper penny, which he made smooth by rubbing it on the brickwork of his cell.

Using a small nail, he engraved the following text:

"When you read this, remember me,
    and bear me in your mind.
    Let all the world say what they will,
    And prove to me in kind."

and he signed it, 'Nathaniel Barton, September 11th 1848'.

CONVICT LOVE TOKENS

Between 1788 and 1868 more than 160,000 men, women and children were transported to Australia, among them over 2,000 of the Parkhurst boys. Expelled from the known world, the majority of these convicts were destined never again to see their loved ones – wives, children or parents. In part to while-away the time while held aboard prison hulks and in institutions like Parkhurst Prison, waiting their turn to make the voyage 'down-under', but also to provide a kind of farewell 'postcard', the convicts began to fabricate 'forget-me-not' keepsakes for their families – love tokens. These conveyed a variety of messages of hope, fear and endearment.

They were made by defacing old 'cartwheel' pennies, removing the King's head from one side and Britannia from the other, to leave a smooth surface, 36 m.m. in diameter, on which they engraved words and pictures by a variety of techniques. The tokens reveal a high level of literacy, even a measure of articulate expression, from among those who were commonly presented as ignorant and ill-bred rogues and villains.

Hundreds of convict love tokens still exist, many on display in public institutions in the United Kingdom and in Australia: British Museum, London; Hull Museum, Yorkshire; Launceston Art Gallery, Cornwall; National Museum of Wales, Cardiff; Powerhouse Museum, Sydney; Queen Victoria Museum, etc.

A significant number of Parkhurst love tokens are known to have existed. There is the love token made by Nathaniel Barton, described in Chapter One of this book. The Parkhurst Heritage Group would like to acquire others to put on display at the Heritage Centre.

FURTHER READING: *Convict Love Tokens* edited by Michelle Field and Timothy Millett.

CHAPTER TWO

Brief Early History and a Few Personalities

IT IS known that in 1798 there was a Military Hospital and Medical Asylum for the children of Soldiers on the site of the present prison. It stayed as a hospital until early 1838 when, by an order from Her Majesty Queen Victoria, it was to be converted into a prison for children. Work started soon after, and the prison opened its doors for the first time on Boxing Day 1838, when it received 102 boys up to the age of fifteen. It would have been a vast improvement on the accommodation the boys were then used to, as they had all been previously incarcerated on the rotting prison ship named *York*, which had been moored in the Solent.

Parkhurst was originally opened "to provide a prison in which Young Offenders may be detained and corrected and receive such discipline as shall appear most conducive to their reformations

The prison ship York *moored in Portsmouth Harbour. Convicts can be seen going aboard.*

and to the repression of crime". The intention was also for it to be used as a form of waiting or holding establishment for boys who were destined to be transported to Australia.

The first Governor was Robert Woolcombe, a retired officer of the Royal Artillery. He had gained previous experience of training boys, before he enlisted into the Army, when employed on a private estate. He had more or less a free hand in picking his staff and it was therefore no surprise when he chose mostly former soldiers from his old Regiment. He certainly made a good choice, for his staff soon built up a good reputation in the local area and they were highly thought of by the prison authorities for their dedication to duty. The main characteristics Woolcombe was looking for in the staff he hired were:

– They had to lead the boys, rather than stand back and drive them.

– They had to take a close personal interest in the boys.

– And they had to strictly enforce the rules, and make certain that they were carried out to the letter.

By an official over-sight the staff had to buy their own uniforms. The uniforms consisted of a military style flat-topped cap, blue frocked-coat with a crown and a letter 'P' on the collar, and all buttons were embossed with 'Parkhurst Prison'.

A Victorian warder with two young charges. Though this photograph was taken at HMP Kingston, Portsmouth, the boys and warders at Parkhurst would have been much the same.

Uniforms of the officers and prisoners at Parkhurst.
(Illustrated London News)

When dressed, the Warders looked very smart, and went about their daily duties with an air of authority.

Being ex-military, Woolcombe also wanted to wear a form of uniform himself. He had already decided that he could adapt the Warders' frock-coat, and include on it, gilded buttons, epaulettes and a dress sword. He wrote to the then Home Secretary, Lord John Russell, asking permission, but received in reply a very resounding 'No'!

Robert Woolcombe received £400 per annum (£28,000 by today's values) as his salary, plus a rent-free house. He also received a quantity of coal and candles. This, together with his military half pay, gave him a reasonable standard of living.

The Prison Chaplain at that time was one of the most important men in the establishment. Often he would be called upon to officiate during the absence of the Governor. He certainly carried a lot authority, as there are cases where early release dates were vetoed on the say-so of the Chaplain. The Rev. Thomas England, MA, was the first appointed Chaplain at Parkhurst and he was paid £250 per year (£17,500 by today's values) and provided with a rent-free house. Scrutiny of local maps of this period reveals that the Chaplain's house was in fact situated adjacent to the cattle barns, in the farm area that was close to the prison's present day north-west boundary, which probably explains why it was allocated free in the first place.

Unfortunately for the Surgeon, his remuneration was only £50 per annum (£3,500 by today's values). For this paltry sum he had to attend the prison between 8 a.m. and 12 noon daily and he had to be on call for any receptions or emergencies as they happened. He was the General Practitioner to all staff and families and, because some of these staff lived two miles away from the prison, he had also to keep a horse and pay for its stabling.

One of the earliest journals we have at the prison is that written by Surgeon Benjamin Browning. Indeed, the first entry is written just five days after the prison opened. In it the Surgeon is constantly asking for a pay rise. In one letter he writes: "In that the pay received, £50 per annum, is much less than that of the cook or his subordinates. Another striking difference is the cook and his subordinates have the added advantage of homes found for them,

The prison dormitories in 'C' Ward were originally communal but due to the unruly conduct of some inmates they were separated into single units with thin deal partitions.
(Illustrated London News)

including coal, candles and rations. Where as I, with the professional responsibilities attached to my job, am not able to enjoy a single one of these advantages." He had a good point and, more importantly, the Home Office accepted his complaint and soon afterwards increased his yearly pay to £150. What the surgeon had omitted to inform the authorities, however, was that, as an ex naval officer, he was drawing half pay, and he also ran his own private practice in Newport. During the years 1842 and 1843, the Governor, Robert Woolcombe, started to take long periods of sick leave. Surgeon Browning recommended seawater bathing, a popular treatment in its day, as a cure for his arthritis. This did not work, though, and Woolcombe retired in July 1843 on health grounds. He collected a gratuity of, quote, "only £400 from a reluctant Treasury"! A few years later he died of tuberculosis.

Not long after the Governor had retired, Surgeon Browning also retired from the prison so that he could attend his private practice more regularly. Very little is known about his successor, a fellow called Benjamin Jemmett, who was by all accounts an early student of The London University. He was the prison doctor for six years, until 1849, when he left to be a General Practitioner in Taunton, Somerset.

We do know a little more of the history of the next doctor. His name was George Henry Dabbs and he came to Parkhurst after serving as doctor on board the prison hulks. There he had received a commendation for his devotion to duty during the cholera epidemic that raged through the prison ships in 1848. So dedicated was he that he refused to set foot ashore until the disease had been vanquished, even though he knew he ran the risk of becoming one of its victims. His sense of hearing had been severely impaired when an inmate, armed with a blunt weapon, attacked him. Shortly after this incident, he was transferred to Parkhurst. He served there for twelve years but nothing more is known of him after he retired.

George Hall was arguably the person who did the most good in the prison. At the time of his appointment to Governor in 1843 he was a Captain in the 52nd Light Infantry, the Duke of Richmond's Regiment. While serving with the regiment, he married the daughter of Colonel Gawler who was also an officer of the 52nd Light Infantry. In applying for the appointment at Parkhurst, he had as his main referee the Chief Commissioner of the Police for the Metropolis, Sir Charles Rowan, who by a strange coincidence was also a previous officer of the 52nd Light Infantry. George Hall was Governor at Parkhurst for twenty years, which makes him the longest serving Governor ever at the prison.

Hall 'invented' the system of Borstal, a system that was well ahead of its day, in which the emphasis was placed on vocational training to provide inmates with a skilled trade. It was adopted officially over fifty years later when the first such purpose-built institution for young offenders was opened. Situated on the banks of the River Medway in Kent, just south-east of Rochester, it took the name Borstal from the village in which it was erected.

When George Hall was appointed Governor at Parkhurst, there were 423 boys serving time in the prison. He soon introduced larger rations, with a daily issue of meat, which rapidly improved the general health of his charges. Overall the prison regime was made a lot easier under George Hall. It remained strict, but it was considerably better than it had been under the previous Governor. Hall also limited the working day to seven hours, a fact not missed by the social reformers of the time.

The Dining Hall in the General Ward. Note that the boys stood up while eating.

(Illustrated London News)

Possibly, too, he was the first official to introduce the 'progressive regime' which is discussed in more detail later. It is a basic fact of life that people will act in a far better manner if they know that there will be a reward for good behaviour. Lose the good behaviour and you lose the reward. Very simple, but effective. Ask any parent!

By grading the boys into First, Second and Third Class prisoners, according to their behaviour, he would pay them the following wages:

First Class Prisoners   –   Sixpence a week

Second Class Prisoners   –   Three pence a week

Third Class Prisoners   –   Nothing at all

That simple scale was the only incentive offered to stay on one's best behaviour. Not surprisingly there is still a form of 'progressive regime' at Parkhurst today, and it still works!

In the year 1853 the transportation of boys was discontinued and the following year, 1854, saw the Reformatory Act become law, allowing privately run reformatories to open up all over the country. This early form of privatisation resulted in a drop in the inmate population at Parkhurst. Morale amongst the staff was severely undermined as the number of inmates fell almost daily. It was inevitable that staff would be laid off. The future of the establishment looked very bleak indeed. Two years later, in 1856, the prison received its first short-term, adult male prisoners, serving terms of three to five years. By 1859, only 25% of the prison population were boys.

The Home Office warned the Governor, Captain Hall, that he should shortly prepare to receive a considerable number of female convicts from the Millbank Gaol in London. This saddened Hall, as he was extremely proud of his boys and what he had achieved with them in almost twenty years. He knew that a great majority of them were to be sent to Dartmoor, simply to make room for the females. He was also concerned about the Reformatory Act of 1854, which allowed privately run reformatories to open up all over the country. Hall could see that all he had worked for would soon disappear, never to return.

In March of 1863, under the care of Lady Superintendent Mrs

Sarah Wilson, a large contingent of female inmates arrived at the prison. Great care was taken to ensure that the remaining boys were kept segregated from the women but the records show that the wooden partition boards were not always entirely successful in this regard. Hall was now left with just seventy-eight boys but the writing was on the wall for, just over a year later, the final order came to send the remaining boys to Dartmoor. Ironically, it was on All Fools Day, 1st April 1864, that the wagons were loaded and the last of the juveniles to serve time at Parkhurst left the prison.

So it was, after twenty years of devoted service, George Hall decided to retire from the service life. In his time at Parkhurst he had changed many bad practices for the better. He had introduced a healthier diet, he gained permission to start agricultural training, and he made the prison regime easier generally, improving the living and working conditions for both his staff and his inmates.

In his long commission as a Prison Governor, Hall had served the local community, the Directors of the Convict Prison, the Home Office, and Her Majesty Queen Victoria herself, but all to little avail, for he received no official recognition of his services and he received no official honours.

Sadly, he was allowed to fade into civilian life, taking with him only a handsome ormolu clock presented to him by the Parkhurst staff. Later he took holy orders before finding a position as Superintendent in a children's home in North London. He died suddenly, four years later, at the relatively young age of fifty-seven.

CHAPTER THREE

Our Royal Visitor, the Women's Riots and a Baby

FOR EVERY single visitor who walks through the gates of a prison, their names are recorded in the Gate-lodge book. Queen Victoria was no exception for when she visited the prison, on Saturday, 2nd August 1845, her name was duly recorded in the book.

Of course she was not alone during the visit, being accompanied by her husband Albert, the Prince Consort. Other dignitaries in the party were the Countess of Charlemont, Sir J. Graham (the Secretary of State for the Prison Service), Major General Wemys who was the Equerry to Her Majesty, Colonel Wylde, the Equerry to The Prince Consort, and finally W. Crawford Esq., who belonged to the office of the Privy Council and who was a regular, official visitor of the prison.

Her Majesty was most impressed with the turnout and manner of the young inmates. They were very polite and, when asked to sing the National Anthem, they sang with such voice that Her Majesty was quite moved. As a reward for their performance she ordered the free pardoning of two of the boys and those lucky two were released the very next morning. The visit did impress the Queen, and she thanked the Governor, George Hall, for all the hard work put in by himself, his staff and, of course, the boys.

The Queen visited a second time in 1863. By then, the rôle of the establishment had changed considerably. Most of the prison now housed the women convicts who had only recently arrived from the Millbank Gaol in London. Only 78 juvenile prisoners remained in Parkhurst, all the others having been moved to Dartmoor a few weeks earlier. George Hall was still the Governor, and his Deputy was the same George Shirlaw who had so distinguished himself caring for the young inmates during the fire in August 1850, thirteen years earlier.

Queen Victoria again visited the juvenile quarter of the prison and, once more, she was impressed with all she saw, although on

The Gate lodge-book entries for Queen Victoria and the Royal party from Osborne House who first visited Parkhurst on Saturday, 2nd August 1845.

this occasion she did not use her powers to pardon anyone. Unfortunately, the women convicts did not behave in the same manner as the boys. As soon as Her Majesty walked into the female compound, they began to catcall from the cell windows. Worse was to follow as the women refused to sing the National Anthem and then turned their backs on the Queen, the ultimate insult. The Queen cut short her visit, much to the embarrassment of the prison officials. We like to think that it was as she left the prison that she uttered those immortal words, now attributed to her: "We are not amused". Unlikely, probably, but she must have said them somewhere! So upset was she reported to be that she gave her Government an order forbidding any other member of the Royalty from ever visiting a prison again.

Back at the prison there was a lot of unrest among the women convicts. It should be remembered that they had only recently been moved down together from London, so they had not completed a settling in period, always a problem time in any penal establishment.

It is recorded that these women convicts were of a depraved

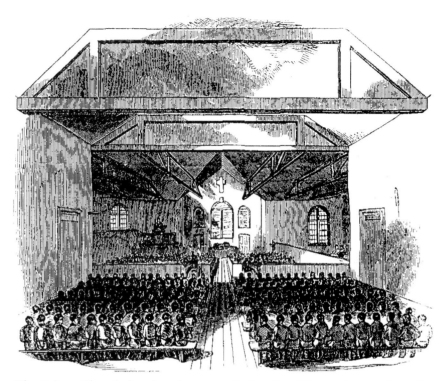

The Prison Chapel showing the segregated ranks of boy prisoners from the 'A', 'B' and 'C' divisions of the General Ward, from the Junior Ward of the Upper Prison and from the Probationary Ward.

(Illustrated London News)

manner and that they had decided to celebrate Queen Victoria's visit with a mutiny. Collectively they smashed windows, shattered crockery and furniture. Eventually, they forced their way out into one of the yards, where, surprisingly, many of them then stripped naked and smothered themselves in tallow grease. The Lady Superintendent, Mrs Sarah Wilson, appealed to George Hall for assistance to deal with the mutineers but so disgusted was he at the behaviour of these women that he refused point blank to give her help. Hall advised Sarah Wilson that she and her female Warders should assert their authority immediately or they would never be able to control the women in the future.

At this, Mrs Wilson tried again to rally her staff to quell the mutiny but they refused, saying that it was too dangerous. When

Female convicts at work during the enforced silent hour.

the pandemonium was at its height, Governor Hall relented and ordered a squad of boys to bring up the fire hose to where the female convicts were and to train it on them. This drastic method, which was used frequently in other jails to control disturbances, cooled the fervour of the majority of the mutineers who returned to their cells. The exception was the group of naked prisoners who preferred to stay on the yard.

These women, drenched and screaming, still refused to leave the area when ordered to do so. Again the female Warders declined to approach the prisoners as they still considered it to be too dangerous. The Deputy Governor, George Shirlaw, then took charge of the situation and gathered a party of his male officers together for the purpose of rushing the women. However, because of the nakedness of these female prisoners, Shirlaw ordered that only married men were to take part in the operation. These hardy but nervous fellows advanced on the naked women, holding outstretched blankets before them. Flinging the blankets over the convicts, they bodily carried them kicking and screaming back to their cells where they were unceremoniously dumped.

In April 1863, a certain Elizabeth Lockwood was sentenced to three years incarceration for common prostitution. She arrived at Parkhurst in the July of the same year. By then she was three months pregnant.

A few weeks after Elizabeth's arrival, Parkhurst experienced its second mutiny, again orchestrated by the female convicts. A faction of very disruptive prisoners had somehow fastened themselves in their cells, from where they kept up such a screaming din it could be heard a considerable distance from the prison. Typically, the Wardresses again refused to approach the prisoners for fear of their own safety. George Hall was once more called upon to assist and again he gallantly came to the rescue. He simply took his master key, opened each cell individually and spoke to all the convicts, one by one. Gradually the situation was calmed, and Mr Hall returned to his own duties, no doubt with a satisfied smile upon his face.

These two incidents provide us with an opportunity to correct a mistruth promoted by an ex convict at the time, who managed to have her views published in the newspapers. Like all views

The squad which quelled the women's riot. Governor George Hall is the gentleman wearing the top hat. George Shirlaw, the Deputy Governor, is the man wearing the light-coloured suit with, to his left, George Butterworth. Eighth from the left is the Chief Infirmary Officer, Charles George Clarke.

expressed by former prisoners, hers was typically sensationalized to make the end result more melodramatic and appealing to readers. This particular, former convict was extremely un-sympathetic towards the penal system as a whole. She stated that the two recent outbreaks of ill discipline at Parkhurst had been due entirely to the severity of the system operated by the 'New Governor'. This allegation could not have been further from the truth for Hall had proved himself, on numerous occasions, to be a Governor who, although strict, was fair in his dealings with both his staff and his charges.

Born in prison soon after this latest fracas, Elizabeth Lockwood's child died when aged just six months. The Death Register entry does not give a cause of death, nor does it give the child's name. That child was the youngest person ever to die at Parkhurst. Anne Smith, another inmate, also lost her child, aged only nine months, in the same year. This child succumbed to a condition recorded as hydrocephalus, a disease of the nervous system frequently associated with cases of Spina Bifida. Sadly, life expectancy in Victorian times was not at all long for the population as a whole and this was mirrored in the confined life within the prison. Thus, it is not surprising to learn that for all deaths of women recorded in the prison register that occurred between 1863 and 1869 the average age was only 32 years. The oldest mortality recorded was of a woman of 55; the youngest, barely more than a girl, aged only 21.

In Victorian times, women who gave birth in prison while under sentence were allowed to keep their child with them, but for only one year. This was to allow the mother to feed the baby naturally. Once the year was up, if the mother still had time to serve, the baby would either have been put up for adoption, sent to a children's home or, more usually, handed over to the mother's family.

Early in 1869, Lady Superintendent Mrs Wilson was informed officially that the female prison rôle of Parkhurst would shortly be coming to an end. She petitioned the local Member of Parliament and lobbied the House of Commons to reverse the decision, but to no avail. A few months later, she and all her staff and prisoners were transferred to a brand new purpose-built female prison at Woking, Surrey.

Prisoners subject to long sentences have an almost limitless amount of time and opportunity available to them to plot escapes or disruptive action inside the prison or to fabricate implements. They can mentally scrutinise all the likely scenarios they may encounter that could lead to the exposure of their plans, permitting them to cover their tracks most effectively. Prison Officers, on the other hand, do not have the benefit of such a luxury, their time being fully occupied with the duties of each shift. Thus, the prisoners have a significant advantage over their custodians.

Two wooden guns, both made with escape in mind but both recovered before they could be used. These date from the 1970s. Another gun was fashioned by carving the shape from a block of soap and then coating it with boot black.

Aided by the criminal minds that led to their arrest, trial and incarceration in the first place, some prisoners are masters of deception and ingenuity. They are able to fashion escape tools, weapons and other gadgets – in Parkhurst and another prison, sophisticated battery-operated tattoo equipment was somehow assembled – from the most innocent materials.

Modularity was often the key to these efforts, attesting to the maxim that the value of the end product was invariably greater than the sum of the individual parts.

Shown on these three pages are a few examples, courtesy of Parkhurst Prison.

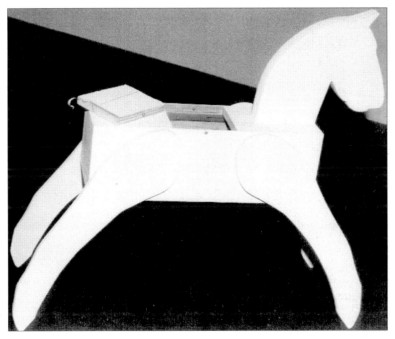

This rocking horse, on the face of it an innocent child's toy, had a secret compartment that was used to store contraband.

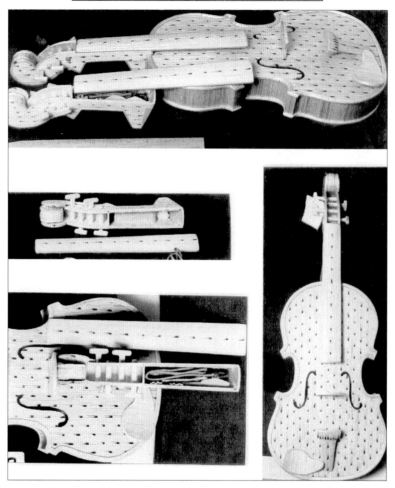

The product of an apparently innocent pastime, this ornamental violin made by a prisoner from match-sticks proved to be a very clever place to hide contraband. It was discovered to contain escape equipment comprising a set of plastic keys, a watch and a length of electric wire. The hiding place was so well concealed that it stood the test of several inspections. A subsequent search of the offender's cell revealed more contraband, sufficient to make a large incendiary device.

CHAPTER FOUR

More About the Doctor

HE OLDEST journal at Parkhurst, as mentioned earlier, is the
book that was kept by Surgeon Benjamin Browning, an ex
Royal Naval Surgeon, who was appointed as the prison's
first doctor. The earliest entry written in the book is a letter dated
31st December 1838, just five days after the prison opened
officially. In this letter the Doctor is informing the Governor that
the flannels issued to the juvenile inmates were causing rheumatic
pains and weakening of the loins. Apparently, the boys were not
used to wearing this type of material next to the skin. His 'cure' for
this complaint was to ask the Governor for a supply of flannel
waistcoats, otherwise called Banyans in the Royal Navy. He also
asked for some elastic belts, called Cholera Belts, as issued to the
military and the Royal Marines during the most recent cholera
epidemic. Whether this absurd request was granted is not known.

The types of punishment meted out upon the boys are generally well documented. There was, however, one form of
imposition that was not widely mentioned, this being the bread
and water diet. If this punishment was awarded, then, by necessity, the prisoner would have required to be visited daily by the
prison doctor. Browning refers to this in another letter sent to the
Governor, dated 9th February 1839. In it he writes: "After my
official visit to the four prisoners kept in solitary confinement on a
ration of bread and water, I am of the opinion that the quantity of
bread allowed daily to these boys is not sufficient for their
support, for the time they are to be confined. In consequence of the
sudden decline of their accustomed supply of meats and potatoes,
and all four inmates being strongly growing lads, above 14 years
of age, I would therefore recommend an extra 4 oz of a pound of
bread, to be supplied to each prisoner per day".

One of the problems encountered in those days was the ignor-
ance of the young prisoners concerning their own birth dates. On
several occasions the doctor was asked to give his opinion as to the
age of the inmate. Again he writes: "In compliance with your
request as to my opinion of prisoner W. Bridges age, I beg to

The Exercise Yard.

acquaint you, that on examination of his person I believe him to be about 18 years of age".

Bridges' name is mentioned in other letters written by another doctor by the name of Robert Blorpan who, when writing a report to the Marquis of Normandy, explains that he is standing in for the prison doctor for a period of ten days. He states that Bridges has been diagnosed as an epileptic and that the young prisoner had experienced his first attacks earlier, when he was at Worcester Jail. Having attended to this young man's medical needs for ten days he was of the opinion that Bridges should not be attended by other prisoners during his frequent fits. The stand-in doctor also brought to the attention of the authorities the fact that other inmates, who were suffering the same ailments as Bridges, could not be admitted to the prison hospital, simply because the hospital was not large enough to accommodate them all.

These comments must have irritated Doctor Browning for, on his return to Parkhurst, he wrote to the Marquis of Normandy a full and comprehensive report of the complete medical history of

The Black Hole, located in the Victorian punishment cells. Periods of solitary confinement in the Black Hole were a regular form of punishment of the child inmates, the longest spell inside lasting nine days. The opening in the middle of the floor was for sanitation purposes.

young Bridges. Whether this was written to combat any repercussions from the previous correspondence is not known, but if so, then I should imagine that Browning would have been a lot more careful about the choice of who substituted for him in the future.

Part of the prison doctor's duties was to examine those poor unfortunates who were destined to be transported to either Perth, Western Australia or to Tasmania (Van Diemen's Land, as it was then known). When one such lad, John Brookes, was examined in 1842, just prior to his departure, the doctor noted that he was in good health and in a fit state to travel. As an afterthought, he added: "Days earlier the prisoner's eyes had become weak and inflamed which were also detected to arise from artful means, and they still look watery and irritated now. In all probability, induced by frictions with his hands, and rubbing in white wash, removed from the walls of his prison cell." Again, we can only surmise, but it would appear that young Brookes was endeavouring to put off that inevitable and terrible sea voyage, though quite in vain as it turned out.

Some of the early treatments used to cure the various maladies of the Victorian era seem, by today's standards, to be either silly or frightening depending, I suppose, on whether you view it from the perspective of the doctor or the patient. The comments here are certainly not intended to belittle the efforts of the medical men of that period who deserved admiration for the dedication to their profession with such limited medical knowledge.

Certainly, Browning was a good conscientious doctor who had the welfare of his charges upper-most in his mind. In the next letter documented here, his concern is especially noticeable as he asks to have a young prisoner reprieved from a punishment. He writes: "Sir, Prisoner A. McIndoe at present in close confinement in the Refractory Ward on bread and water as per the Secretary of State's order for 28 days, has been labouring under Retention of Urine, which requires a daily introduction of a catheter to draw it off, frequently, twice a day. From pain and other effects of the complaints, the prisoner is becoming weak and reduced, and the pain at the neck of the bladder is severe every time the fluid is drawn off. The prisoner has had an increase of bread since the start of his punishment, but I am of the opinion that he should have a more nutritious diet, and be moved to the infirmary for the restoration of his health."

I shall leave you to draw your own conclusions on the merits of increasing bread rations as a cure for a bladder problem!

Before closing this chapter, I would like to mention a particular, double-paged return drawn up by the doctor on the request of the Governor Woolcoombe. The return comprised of a list detailing all the juvenile inmates who were registered as sick during the year 1841. From this meticulous record, we know that prisoner no. 153 went on the sick list just once in that year whereas prisoner 173 troubled the infirmary eight times. Unfortunately, the document does not indicate the reasons for this difference. The grand total of those on the sick list, so the doctor informs us, was 505 for the reporting period, a number of sickness cases that is sub-divided into 33 different diseases or medical conditions.

Surprisingly the common cold is not mentioned, although the symptoms are – for example, there were 25 cases of sore throats and 41 cases of catarrh. Some 22 inmates were treated for accidental damage (whatever that was?), thirteen for rheumatism and, perhaps not surprisingly, a mighty 133 for chilblains. Cold feet seem to have been a common problem for the boys, especially for one unfortunate who was diagnosed as having frost bite on his heels. Mind you he was probably better off than the lad who was diagnosed with piles!

Perhaps most striking, is the total absence of mention of any of the killer diseases of that era – Small Pox, Diphtheria, Typhoid Fever and so on – even though in the wider, local population there were isolated occurrences, even significant outbreaks of these illnesses.

Finally, we return to the case of the young man, mentioned earlier, who had a problem with urine retention. Again the doctor writes: "I have to report that prisoner A. McIndoe, whose case was especially reported recently, for your information I am recommending his removal from the prison at the earliest possible period. He is this day labouring under great and violent excitements amounting to delirium, in consequence of which I have deemed it necessary, under the authority of the 115th Rule of the Parkhurst Prison Regulations, to call in additional medical assistance, which I have done in the person of Mr Tulliett who is in charge of the Pauper Lunatics in the House of Industry [an establishment that was originally located in the grounds of the present day St Mary's Hospital]."

Mr Tulliett, himself, wrote about the case a couple of days later. He totally agreed with Browning's diagnosis and concludes his entry by saying: "'I consider the prisoner to be labouring under nervous excitement with no inflammation of the brain, but that this case is one of danger".

The young man's health deteriorated rapidly and a Removal Order was issued for the inmate to be transferred to the *Bruton*, a Convict Hospital Ship moored at Gosport. Nevertheless, Doctor

Names of Diseases which have occurred during the year 1841.

Diseases.	No. of Cases	Diseases.	No. of Cases
		Brought forward	190
Fevers	2	Painful discharge of Urine	1
Ophthalmia	20	Worms	1
Inflammation of Lungs	2	Dropsical Swelling	1
Ear aches	2	Scrophula	2
Headaches	16	Consumption	1
Sore Throats	25	Swelled Glands	2
Rheumatism	13	Whitlows	9
Inflammations (common or simple)	7	Abscesses	29
Scarlatina	3	Boils	35
Piles	1	Accidents & Wounds	22
Catarrhs	41	Scalds & Burns	15
Indigestion	3	Ulcers	13
Palpitation of Heart	1	Scald Heads	23
Epilepsy	6	Itch & Cutaneous Eruptions	27
Colica	4	Frost Bitten Feet	1
Bowel Complaints	42	Chilblains	133
Involuntary discharge of Urine	2		
Total	190	Grand total	505

31st Decr 1841.

Benjn Browning M.D.
Surgeon —

A page from Dr Benjamin Browning's journal, summarising the diseases which were recorded during 1841, a total of 505 cases ranging from minor (indigestion) to quite serious (consumption) ailments. It is, perhaps, not surprising that the commonest complaint was chilblains.

Browning considered the inmate to be in too delicate a condition to be moved, so he remained at Parkhurst. In his monthly report to the Secretary of State he declares that prisoner McIndoe was "very emaciated, rendering his ultimate recovery doubtful".

Young Archibald McIndoe died in the late afternoon of 10th April 1842. He had been extremely weak for several days previously and an attack of bronchitis terminated his short life. A Coroner's Inquest was held the day after his death, which returned the verdict "that the said Arch. McIndoe, departed this life on 10th April 1842, by the visitation of God, of Natural Disease, to wit of inflammation of the Bronchial, and not by any violent means whatever".

Benjamin Browning's last entry in these fascinating journals is a routine entry, a monthly report to the Secretary of State in which he makes no mention of the fact that he is approaching the end of his appointment at Parkhurst. He does, however, mention that, because of the recent cold and snowy weather, the cases of chilblains are on the rise!

CHAPTER FIVE

Through the Turn of the Century

THE WOMEN'S PRISON finally came to a close in the middle part of 1869 with the departure of Lady Superintendent Mrs Sarah Wilson, her staff, and the troublesome female prisoners who were ordered to the brand new purpose-built women's prison at Woking.

So now the boys had gone and the females had gone, and the big question was what would happen to this valuable and important establishment? The answer was that Parkhurst now became a male convict prison, primarily to house short-term prisoners – that is, those with a sentence of three to five years. But in these inmates the prison began to collect an increasing population of mentally unstable and physically handicapped inmates which presented the prison with unique problems. The changes introduced by the authorities closed what was arguably the most important era in the history of Parkhurst – the Victorian era that in some respects forged the way ahead for the modern prison service.

With the present-day service undergoing almost constant change, it is not unreasonable to wonder what the original staff – George Hall, Captain Woolcombe and their colleagues – would think of our methods today. Not much, we suspect. It would be wrong to suggest that there has ever been other than an absolute commitment to the best operation of Parkhurst but, in my opinion, those early officials believed wholeheartedly in what they were doing and, most importantly, they were convinced that firm discipline was the only basis on which to build a system aimed at reformation.

The Reverend John Spear, in charge of the Junior Ward, wrote in 1848: "While kindness and persuasion is the prevailing law in this institution, punishment is not dispensed with, and therefore obedience is the safest and happiest path for them to walk on". In spite of all our modern refinements – our weakness for wrapping up truths in psychological and sociological jargon – those early Victorians, and in some cases, their methods, still have much to teach us.

The Lunatic Asylum, Parkhurst – a general view in Victorian times showing supervised work parties digging in the foreground, with the prison on the right. (Illustrated London News)

In 1877 an Act of Parliament was passed which transferred the control of prisons to the Home Secretary from the local Justices. Five Prison Commissioners were appointed to oversee all prison establishments, to ensure they were being run fairly and properly. For the first time all prisons came under the same administration. In 1881 the Prison Commissioners announced that the number of

The exterior of 'B' Wing, seen from the rear – a more recent picture.

prisons throughout the country would be cut from 113 to 67, which meant a substantial reduction of the staff in the Service.

Just before the turn of the 20th century, the general public was becoming increasingly concerned about the running of the contemporary prison system, so much so that Mr Herbert Gladstone was appointed to set up a series of departmental committees to try to identify the underlying problems. The Gladstone Report, which was published in 1895, is still considered to this day as being one of the most important and far reaching documents in the history of the Prison Service.

From this point, the Parkhurst story becomes rather fragmented and even, perhaps, insignificant. The Victorian era of the prison is well documented, mainly because this particular period contained so much of interest that was worthy of being recorded. Looking back, it seems that, from the beginning of the 20th century the prison just went about its business with the minimum of fuss and, as a consequence, little of a dramatic nature occurred to attract the attention of the outside world.

We do know, however, that, because of the Gladstone Report, a separate area was built, adjacent to the prison (in Nicholson Street, off Horsebridge Hill, Newport) to serve as a lunatic asylum. This relieved the main prison of the burden of having to mix sane and insane prisoners together on the same landings. One of our better and, indeed, bigger journals in the prison is the record of these lunatics – their social, criminal, and medical history.

Apart from this, little is known of this part of the establishment, except that the officers on duty around this time were issued with a small stave or stick, to be used only in the act of defence, should the need arise. Although this stick is only ten inches long, it certainly packs a punch as it has been hollowed out and filled with lead!

I suppose that here would be a good place to correct a very popular misconception about Parkhurst Prison. Over the last few years the establishment has gone through a massive building programme, which has completely refurbished the old, dark, Victorian interiors of the buildings, creating something that is now a lot brighter, cleaner, and more importantly safer, not only for the prisoners but, of course, for the staff.

Parkhurst interior view – a landing in the old Segregation Unit under 'B' Wing.

It was while the various contractors were ripping up the old floorboards in 'B' Wing that they discovered an old canvas bag full of sand. Immediately, the word went around that the bag used to test the gallows had been found. According to rumours the gallows were originally located at the far end of 'C' Wing and I do agree that this particular place is large enough for an execution area. However, to set the record straight once and for all, Parkhurst was never a hanging jail. It was always intended, initially, to be a prison for the retention of inmates destined to be transported to Australia. Later, when it changed to an all male adult prison (in 1869), it housed only habitual prisoners known to the service as PDs (preventative detention).

The crime that was automatically given the death sentence (amongst others) was, of course, murder. All prisoners under this

One of the prison workshops.

Interior view of the Special Secure Unit (SSU) where the Great Train Robbers and the Krays were held. Drying laundry draped upon the railings at each level gave the Wing a distinctively pungent aroma. The netting between the galleries served two purposes – it prevented suicide attempts and it also acted as a barrier if prisoners aimed missiles at officers on lower levels.

sentence would be sent to a hanging jail, there to await either the execution or, if they were lucky, the successful appeal. The only murderers serving time in Parkhurst would have been those who were diagnosed as criminally insane, held in the Lunatic Asylum, or, indeed, those who had appealed successfully and whose death penalty had been commuted to life imprisonment.

On reading through the Lunatic Asylum Register, one cannot help but make comparisons between the sentences given just after the turn of the century and those imposed today. One of the commonest crimes back in those days was stack firing or, to give it a more modern name, arson, for which the guilty offender could expect a sentence of between three to six years. Other crimes were dealt with just as firmly, albeit disproportionately; for instance, one inmate charged with carnally knowing a girl of under sixteen who was given a term of fourteen years, whereas another offender was sentenced to fifteen years for impairing the current gold coin of the realm with intent, possibly an early case of a crime against the state being treated more seriously than a crime against the person.

All the original assessments written in the Lunatic Asylum register were recorded by the Medical Officer of the time, a gentleman by the name of O. F. H. Treadwell. Some of his comments raise a smile nowadays, although of course, they were written as a proper report, detailing the actions of the inmate. Most were suffering from some form of delusion – one poor misfortunate believed he was a prison officer who was covered in green paint; another was diagnosed as insane, "because of his religious excitement". Some of the excuses for their crimes were just as amazing. No explanation is required for the inmate whose capital penalty was commuted to life imprisonment because his gun went off as he was cleaning it! Another was charged with manslaughter after he "killed his child, by throwing him to the ground, cause, passion, because the child could not keep pace with him whilst on a country tramp".

Unfortunately, today the prisons are full of mentally unstable inmates who have to serve their sentences in prison, simply because there is no room for them in the proper establishments designated for the detention of the mentally unstable (i.e. secure hospitals). It seems that at the turn of the century almost every county had its own Lunatic Asylum for, after a period of time, all the criminally insane held at Parkhurst were transferred to their local county asylums, be it in Stafford, Suffolk, Kent, or any one of the many other institutions around the country. Broadmoor played an important rôle then, as indeed it does today, as an establishment that could care for the more dangerous criminally insane.

Occasionally, of course, inmates were cured and allowed to serve the remainder of their sentence in a normal prison. There are also cases of inmates moving in the opposite direction, from the mainstream prison to an asylum, as changing circumstances dictated.

HONOURING CONVICT HEROES

Extract from the Isle of Wight County Press, Saturday, 2nd April, 1921

HONOURING CONVICT HEROES.

MEMORABLE CEREMONY AT PARKHURST PRISON.

Perhaps the most unique and interesting war memorial in the country is that placed in the Prison Chapel at Parkhurst, which was unveiled on Wednesday by Major-General J. E. B. Seely, C.B., C.M.G., D.S.O., M.P., the lord-lieutenant of Hampshire, for it is a tribute paid by convicts to fellow prisoners who were liberated on volunteering to fight for their country and fell gallantly facing the enemy. The memorial consists of a brass tablet on a dark oak back ground, and the inscription is: "To the glory of God and in memory of those who went out from imprisonment in this place and gave their lives on the Field of Honour in the Great War, 1914-1918. 'These are they which came out of great tribulation,' Rev. vii, 14. Erected by their fellow prisoners."

The Memorial was subscribed for by the convicts only, and so keen were some to give substantial sums towards it that the Governor had to limit the subscriptions. Men of all nationalities, including a German and a Mahommedan, willingly gave their little quota, and judging by the reverence and general demeanour of the 700 or so prisoners who were present at the ceremony, no memorial yet erected has been raised with a more genuine spirit of respect and honour than was this tablet in memory of men who might, not unjustly perhaps, have felt that they had but little to arouse their spirit of patriotism. Yet as the Governor and the gallant General mentioned in the course of their sympathetic and able speeches every man who was able volunteered and amongst the large number who went was one brave man who died of wounds, after winning the highest Honour the British nation can award her heroes of the battlefield – the V.C., whilst several others gained commissions and promotion for gallantry. The raising of this very worthy and unique memorial is another tribute to the humane and tactful treatment of those in this penal establishment by the excellent Governor (Capt. R. Hughes D'Aeth), and his subordinates, and we feel that the prisoners themselves would wish that this public acknowledgement should be made.

On his arrival at the entrance of the chapel Gen. Seely, who was in uniform, was met by a guard of honour formed of Prison officers who had served in the war, and the General shook hands and conversed with each man. He then passed into the chapel where practically the whole of the prisoners were assembled, listening to suitable music played on the organ by Mr. Gaster. Amongst those also present, in addition to Gen. Seely and the Governor, were Mr. Edward Wintle (governor of Camp-hill Prison), Major Dunn, D.S.O., of the Royal Ulster Rifles, Mr. A. E. Scott, M.C. (deputy governor), the Rev. A. F. O'N. Williams (chaplain), the Rev. T. Glaisyer (assistant chaplain), Dr. Slaney (deputy medical officer), and Fathers Ahearn and Watson, of the Roman Catholic Church, Newport. The tablet on the chancel wall was veiled with the Union Jack.

Addressing the company as lads, the Governor said he wished to introduce Major-General Seely, who had done them the great honour of coming to unveil their memorial. The General, as they could see by the medals on his breast, was a distinguished soldier, a keen and active politician who had held the rank of Secretary of State for War, and he came to them as the official representative of H.M. the King, in his position as lord-lieutenant of Hampshire. General Seely and others from outside would perhaps like to know that that memorial had been contributed to by the men only. The officers had had absolutely nothing whatever to do with it. It was a memorial given by the men before them in honour of their comrades who gave their lives for their country. Men of so many different religions and creeds had contributed to it, and were present, that it had been decided to have no religious ceremony.

He did not know exactly how many went to fight for their country, neither did he know for certain how many gave up their lives: but he should like to say that many who were left behind were not so left of their own free will. A great many who volunteered were not allowed to go, for physical and other reasons, but those who had to stay in that establishment during the war worked willingly and to the best of their ability to help their country by making articles used by the Navy and Army, and in the postal services for the troops. He thanked Major Dunn for his presence and for allowing the buglers of the Royal Ulster Rifles to sound the "Last Post".

Gen. Seely said: Capt. D'Aeth and gentlemen, I am very glad to have the privilege of coming here to-day to unveil this most interesting memorial. In the course of my duty as His Majesty's representative in this county it has been my privilege to unveil many war memorials but I think I can say that none is more unique than this one. When the war broke out almost all of you here – so I am told by your distinguished guardian Capt. D'Aeth – volunteered to serve your country. Whatever had happened in the past, you all said then, "Now our country is in danger, we are willing to serve her." That is to the eternal honour of you all, and, alas! some of those who went made the full sacrifice. It is very interesting to know that the memorial has been set up by the perfectly spontaneous contributions of you whom I now address. One of your number received the highest decoration a man can receive – more precious than any of the great and ancient orders which England can bestow on her sons – the Victoria Cross [applause, which was hurriedly subdued]. I do not wonder you wish to applaud it. I wish we could but we are in a house of worship and must necessarily conduct our proceedings in silence. It is no wonder, but natural, that you would wish to applaud that most romantic achievement of a man going from within these walls, who was not at one for the moment with the society to which he belonged, and who won that rare honour, and most distinguished of all honours – the Victoria Cross – for supreme gallantry in the face of the enemy. When I add that I believe that he died of wounds received in that most gallant way, I think you would agree when I say that all of you will be able to look back on the past with mingled feelings, and look forward to the future with hope rising from the thought that one of your number was one of the most distinguished of England's sons.

After referring to the fact that men of all creeds and nationalities, including one who fought with the enemy, had insisted on subscribing to the tablet, the General said they had admired the action of that one man. It reminded him of something that happened to him almost at that exact hour on that day three years ago, when a vast host of men of many races were all trying to do their duty. They would not that day go into the question of who was right or wrong. They could agree that most of those who fought, fought bravely for their cause. March 30, 1918, was, according to Marshal Foch, the most critical moment of the war, when the Austro-German combination had formed a great host and were advancing on Amiens. On that day portions of the Allied armies turned at bay and with devoted and determined valour fought against the host which was endeavouring to divide the Allied armies. He happened to be where some of the heaviest fighting then took place and he would tell them of one incident. He was riding through the Bois de Moreuil, which we had just re-captured. There were many of the enemy inside the wood who had not surrendered, although the British troops had surrounded it, and, as he rode through, he saw a German soldier lying on his back against a tree bleeding from a wound in his neck. There was a lot of shooting going on and he (the General) did not wish to stay in one place too long, so he turned to the wounded man – because hatred between the nations was not found on the battlefield, especially towards an enemy who was out of action – and in his very bad German said "I will send a stretcher-bearer for you". The wounded man immediately reached out for his rifle, "but fortunately for me," added the General, "he could not quite reach it," and he hissed back these wonderful words in German, "No, no; I will die untaken." That was a very brave thing for a wounded man to say, and, unfortunately, it proved true, for, almost as he spoke, a shell came crashing through the trees and he was killed. That showed that courage of the most extreme kind was not confined to one side, and it should make us all the more thankful that victory came our way.

He hoped that God would give us peace in the future. He told them that little story to show that men could rise to that point of courage which enabled them to refuse to surrender even when at the point of death, and he was sure that was the kind of spirit their comrades showed, and which they would be prepared again to show should the need ever arise. "We all have our ups and downs in life," said the General in conclusion. "I have had many myself, but I am quite sure that as the days go by and you return to your ordinary vocations, you will be found doing good and useful work for the community. I hope that you will remember this day, gentlemen, when I, as the King's humble representative, came amongst you to give you this message, and when you commemorated with thankfulness the brave deeds of those who gave their lives for others."

HONOURING CONVICT HEROES

POSTSCRIPT

The prisoner believed to be the anonymous holder of the Victoria Cross, mentioned in the report on the Parkhurst Prison Convict's Memorial which was unveiled and dedicated in 1921, is William Mariner. This was not his original name, though. He changed it before he joined the Army.

William Mariner left Parkhurst Prison to join the 2nd Battalion of the Kings Royal Rifle Corps as a Rifleman. The account of the deed in which he won the highest award for bravery in the face of the enemy, extracted from The Register of the Victoria Cross, is as follows:

"On 22nd May 1915, near Cambrin, France, during a violent thunderstorm, Private Mariner left his trench and crept out through German wire entanglements until he reached the emplacement of an enemy gun which had been hindering progress. He climbed on top of a German parapet and threw a bomb under the roof of the emplacement and, after fifteen minutes, he threw another bomb. He then waited while the guns opened fire on the wire entanglements behind him and eventually he was able to return to his own trench. He had been out alone for one and a half hours."

William Mariner was killed a year later, on 1st July 1916, at the Battle of the Somme. He was thirty-six years old. His name is recorded on the war memorial at Thiepval, France.

As a further postscript to this account of William Mariner, there was another convict at Parkhurst who was awarded the Victoria Cross, although in his case he received it before he was sentenced to serve time in prison. This was Thomas Flynn who is also the subject of a controversy as to who was the youngest person to receive this decoration. Thomas Flynn was fifteen years and 89 days old when he won his Victoria Cross on 28th November 1857 at the Battle of Cawnpore, during the Indian Mutiny. His contender for the youngest V.C. is Andrew Fitzgibbon who was believed to be fifteen years and 100 days old when he was awarded the decoration in 1861.

Thomas Flynn, a Drummer enlisted in the 64th North Staffs Regiment, was awarded the Victoria Cross "for conspicuous bravery in the charge on the enemy's (Indian) guns on 28th November 1857 when, being himself wounded, he engaged in hand-to-hand encounter with two of the rebel artillerymen".

It is surprising that Thomas Flynn did not forfeit his Victoria Cross as, from the day he landed at Dover on his return from India, he spent a considerable amount of his time in prison. In total he completed fourteen Periods of Detention, adding up to 586 days 'inside', including 31 days in Parkhurst in November/December 1868. Thomas Flynn died on 10th August 1892 in the Athlone East Workhouse, when 50 years of age.

CHAPTER SIX

A Lull in the Excitement

PARKHURST'S QUIET period continued. For more than twenty years it seems to have gone into a sort of slumber, quietly getting on with prison life, with nothing, apparently, upsetting the system. Which is, I suppose, a success story in itself, however boring that might be!

The First World War didn't interrupt the prison routine too badly despite the fact that, although the prison officers were in a reserved occupation, many of them volunteered to serve their country in a more patriotic fashion by joining the armed forces. Unfortunately, certain of these officers fell casualties of the conflict and, in 1922, a War Memorial was unveiled in the prison chapel, commemorating the officers who had given their lives in the Great War.

What was not commonly known at the time was that a lot of prisoners were also released early from their sentences, also to serve their country but that is where the similarity ends for, if it was an ex-inmate who was killed in battle, his name was excluded from any form of memorial. This, I am pleased to report, is now being rectified and very soon the names of all those who gave their lives, will be suitably inscribed to afford them the enduring recognition they deserve.

Two prisoners who caused a disturbance at Parkhurst in August 1927 were sent to Dartmoor as a punishment, there to experience a discipline as strict as anywhere in the prison service. One of these inmates gained notoriety before he was removed, by climbing on the chapel roof and remaining there for thirty hours, only coming down when he was threatened with the hose pipe. The other prisoner also caused a disturbance by plunging himself into a tank full of warm tar that was on the exercise yard. These two prisoners had been the main instigators in a night of unrest on the accommodation block when all the inmates kicked their cell doors, broke windows and furniture, and kept up a din all night.

Another disturbance in June 1938, which was just as violent, was triggered for a reason that is quite surprising. Earlier in the

The unique clover-leaf building at the southern end of 'C' Wing.

previous year a plan to get more prisoners into work was started, called the 'work-for-wages' scheme. It was designed to enable inmates to earn more money, by way of a bonus, to pay for such luxuries as tobacco and chocolate. For three prisoners this was an excellent idea, until they were ordered to the infirmary to be treated for minor ailments. This was not viewed as a good move by the authorities, as these three men were anxious to continue working to earn the extra money. They asked to be removed from the hospital and to be allowed to return to the workplace. The request was denied, so the men barricaded themselves in the ward and started to systematically smash the place up. Eventually over-powered by the staff and removed to the Segregation Block, they were dealt with by the visiting magistrate who promptly sacked them from their jobs in the prison! The original idea behind the 'work-for-wages' scheme was to keep the infirmary clear of malin-gerers, to make doctors' parades a thing of the past. It was rather ironic in the event, for the officers certainly cleared out the hospital ward, even if the prisoners were dragged out kicking and fighting!

Three years later, in 1941, and yet another 24 hours of wild disorder marred the history of the establishment. This time it was food that was the cause, possibly the subject of most complaints inside any prison. This incident, which was reported in the *Daily*

East side of the clover-leaf with 'C' Wing extending to the right leading to 'G' Wing and 'B' Wing.

Mail, started in the inmates' dining hall. Apparently, soup was on the menu that particular day but it was not considered to be satisfactory. One prisoner stood up and shouted loudly: "There is no meat in this soup, we are not vegetarians". This was the signal for all the inmates to throw their dinners away, using the unfortunate officers on duty as target practice for their tin mugs, issued to the inmates for other, quite different purposes! The ringleaders were quickly rounded-up and, in time honoured fashion, frog-marched to the Segregation Block.

The disturbance had been quelled but it flared up again at the evening tea meal, and again at breakfast the following day. However, with the ringleaders removed and unable to exacerbate the situation, the disturbances gradually petered out and prison life settled down again into some form of order. In reporting the incident, the *Daily Mail* took the opportunity to inform the general public of a typical daily menu for prisoners:

Breakfast – Bread and butter, porridge and a pint of tea.

Dinner – Corned beef patties, mashed potatoes, beetroot, 2oz of bread, rice pudding and rhubarb and a cup of tea.

Tea – Bread and butter, cheese and a pint of cocoa.

How this compares with the prisoners' diet of just forty years earlier, as revealed in an interesting publication produced at HM Prison Parkhurst in 1902, entitled, *Manual of Cookery for the Use of Prison Officers*. A particularly un-mouth-watering entry is the 'Recipe for Gruel'. Sometimes known as 'Stirabout', gruel was a thin porridge of oatmeal and water that was so basic and lacking in substance it is hard to imagine how it could ever require a recipe. The Manual informs us, as follows:

"Ingredients to produce 1 pint of gruel – 2 oz of coarse oatmeal (Scotch), 1 pint of water, 1/4 teaspoon salt (or 1/2 oz sugar).

Method – Mix the oatmeal in a pan with sufficient cold water to form a paste. Heat up the remainder until it boils and stir to the mixed oatmeal; add the salt and allow it to simmer for at least 20 minutes. It is necessary to stir the mixture occasionally with a wooden spoon or bat, otherwise it is likely to burn!"

Eminently forgettable – which may be why it needed a written recipe – it certainly was not going to win an Egon Ronay award for Parkhurst!

After leaving the prison on completion of their sentence, some former prisoners told one particular newspaper that the inmates were constantly demanding more tea, and that an unofficial prisoners' union has been formed to take this very important grievance to the appropriate authority.

Another incident of agitation broke out in July 1949. It may appear that such disturbances were a regular occurrence at this establishment but that was not really the case, besides the Prison Service categorises these disruptions as mostly trivial, minor affairs. It is the media, trying to expand their circulation, which blows them up out of all proportion. Put very simply, the prison service does not sell newspapers. Therefore, we have disturbances. It is the papers that have riots!

This particular disturbance (riot?) came about when two rival gangs of prisoners realised that they both had the same escape idea and, as neither gang would concede to the other, a full-scale battle ensued. It is not recorded which of the gangs gained the upper hand, but what is for certain is that no-one escaped in the following weeks! However, during this incident the police were tipped-off by the prison that an escape was planned and two

The front side exterior of 'A' and 'D' Wings. The glass-roofed building in the background is the bath-house.

known London criminals were arrested near Ryde railway station and taken in for questioning.

Moving into the next decade, there was a spate of 'slashings' at Parkhurst early in 1952. These extreme punishments are normally reserved for inmates who 'grass' on their fellow prisoners, that is to say those who give information to the authorities about what is happening 'behind the scenes' on the landings. Two prisoners held another inmate, who was serving a six-year sentence for housebreaking, up against the door to his cell, while a third slashed his face. The authorities would, of course, have investigated this incident but, as normal, they would have come up against a complete wall of silence, as no other prisoner would inform for fear of receiving the same treatment. Two days after the attack, another inmate was slashed in similar circumstances but whether the two assaults were connected is not known.

The prison staff had little option but to temporarily lock down the establishment and conduct a very thorough search for the weapons used in the attack. These searches are usually effective. They work because, even if the weapons are not found, the staff know that they will be thrown from the cell window as soon as the inmates realise they are going to be turned over. Over the course of the next six months, all convicts with a short list of convictions were moved to other prisons. This was to make room for more habitual law-breakers. The prison population at the time was 670, of which 480 were categorised as Preventative Detention. It was the remaining 190 ordinary prisoners who were moved elsewhere. This sort of mass move always causes unrest with the prisoners especially those who have settled in the establishment reasonably well. Not only that, more importantly, this form of prisoner management can end up with all the bad apples in the same barrel, a potentially explosive mixture.

CHRISTMAS DINNER, 1961

The daily ration of food is dictated by the budget of the establishment. A good catering officer will scrimp and save over the year to try to gain a few pennies, and give the prisoners a few extras for the Christmas period.

Christmas 1961 was no exception, and breakfast that day consisted of grapefruit, cornflakes, milk, bacon, eggs, frankfurters and tinned tomatoes, with tea, bread and margarine. The dinner was mushroom soup, chicken quarters, roast pork, roast potatoes, Brussells sprouts and gravy, followed by, of course, Christmas pudding with sauce, and coffee. As if this was not enough, tea consisted of pork pie, salad mayonnaise, tea, bread, margarine, fruit trifle and ice cream, and Christmas cake.

The Christmas film was *No Way to Treat a Lady*, and *The Charge of the Light Brigade* was shown on Boxing Day.

CHAPTER SEVEN

Who Guards the Guards?

ACK IN the old days of the prison's history, it was not only the prisoners who managed to find themselves occasionally in hot water. In the early 1930s the staff also had to comply with a reasonably strict code of discipline. The prison officers, who were known collectively as 'blue-shirts', had to be on their constant guard, not only with the demands of looking after the inmates but to ensure they stayed within the bounds of the many rules and regulations.

Failure to observe the Prison Service code of behaviour could sometimes result in the downfall of an officer. Officers accused of breaking the rules were issued with what was commonly known as a 'half-sheet', called this simply because of its size, about half the size of an A4 sheet of paper. The charge against the officer was laid out upon this form, the Report Against An Officer, to give it its correct name.

The accused could then reply to the charges, on the reverse of the form. Eventually, the matter would be brought before the Governor, who would sit in judgement on the case. For the officer this would have been a very worrying time, for the Governor then, just as he does today, had the authority to dismiss his staff.

As an example of this process, revealing how apparently insignificant or innocent actions could lead to disciplinary breaches, a true incident dating from April 1932 is detailed here, using pseudonyms to protect the anonymity of those concerned. Officer John Smith found himself on the wrong end of a half-sheet when he was accused of Highly Improper Conduct while in charge of one of the outside working parties.

The report, which is illustrated, suitably censored, in this chapter, reads as follows:

"Highly improper conduct, when as i/c 27 Garden Party, did allow his men to cease labour before the proper time. Also unauthorised allowing his men to partake of Refreshments (tea etc) at about 3.20 p.m. above date, when visited by the Governor whilst working at the M.O. House."

REPORT AGAINST AN OFFICER.

H.M. Prison, *Parkhurst:* | 22ⁿᵈ *April* 1932

Rank *Officer* Name ██████████████

reported by *P.O.* ████████ for *Highly*

Improper Conduct, when i/c 27. Garden Party. did allow his men to cease labour before the proper time. also unauthorized allowing his men to partake of Refresh. ments (Tea etc) at about 3.20 pm above date. when visited by the Governor. whilst working at the. M.O. House.

Signature ██████████████

Rank *Prin Officer*

Rank *Officer* Name ██████████████

will reply overleaf to this report for the information of the Governor.

~~Deputy, Governor~~ Chief Officer).

A typical example of a 'Report Against An Officer' form, the so-called 'half-sheet', dating from the 1930s. With the exception of the Chief Officer, all the names have been deliberately obliterated.

Officer John Smith replied on the reverse of the form, justifying his actions with the following excuse:

" Sir, I beg to report that I had finished all necessary work at the M.O. Quarters and was supervising the loading of the cart to go to another job. As I was doing so, to my astonishment, Mrs Forsyth herself, personally brought out a tray on which were tea and cakes, and handed the same to 577 Donovan, without my authority or permission. I was remonstrating with her when visited by the Governor. Sir, Please see attached statement."

In the statement Mr John Smith further explained the incident away as follows:

"With reference to my report of April 22nd 1932, I beg to acquaint you with the following facts. On Tuesday the 19th inst, when employed with no. 27 Party, at the house of the Senior Medical Officer, Mrs Forsyth came out and in a general way stated 'Good morning, and how are you all getting on?'. She then went over and spoke to No. 577 J. Donovan. I went across and asked if there was anything she wanted, and she said that she was speaking about some sweet peas and the preparation of a bed. I said 'I am sorry madam, but I am just going away'. Mrs Forsyth said 'Oh, are you, where are you going?' I replied 'To prepare the hut'. She said 'Won't you be coming back?' I then replied that I had my programme arranged for me, by the regular officer i/c of the party. She then went into the house. Donovan then said 'Why didn't you say that we would come up on Friday? I particularly wanted to come up again on Friday.' I told him that I was in charge and that we should not come up. These facts I reported to Principal Officer Jones, who told me that he would make enquiries and let me know what to do. On the 21st inst, I received instructions to arrange to go to the S.M.O.'s residence called 'The Elms'. The P.O. told me he would be about, as they wanted to get to the bottom of things 'once and for all'. I was told to carry on ordinary, and I did. A box of sweet peas were collected and taken to 'The Elms'. The party slowed up towards 11 a.m., evidentially (sic) trying to hang out their time. It was however necessary to go up again after dinner. This I also reported to P.O. Jones. At 3 p.m. instead of the usual arrangements, I ordered the men to load up, Mrs Forsyth then being at the north door of her house, went inside. As I proceeded to load up she came out with a tray, on which were 6 cups, a jug, and some cakes, and handed the same to 577 Donovan. She had not spoken to me and I was very surprised by her actions. I said, 'Excuse me madam, but it would be much more charitable if you would firstly discuss the matter with the officer i/c of the party, who is not allowed to permit such hospitality, and who does not always see eye-to-eye with you in these matters'. She said she was sorry, but it did not occur often, and she only performed such acts 'once in a while'.

"I told her that nevertheless, an officer was held responsible, to ensure that such irregularities did not occur. With that the Governor, came on the scene, and I informed Mrs Forsyth of this fact. I also told Dr Forsyth, that the Governor, when paying his visit, had seen my party receiving hospitality at Mrs Forsyth's expense, without my authority, or consent, and that such a practice was irregular.

"I hope sir, that these facts may be taken into consideration when adjudicating on my report."

The Governor, Captain G. F. Clayton was very interested in John Smith's statement, as he had previously had adverse reports regarding the doctor's wife, and her misplaced hospitality. To investigate this matter further he wrote to the Senior Medical Officer:

"With reference to the attached report against Officer John Smith, I have adjourned the case until I have received a report from you. I should mention that the facts occurring on Tuesday were duly reported to me by P.O. Jones, and that I gave instructions to Officer John Smith, that if he had any suspicions of 577 Donovan, he had better let Donovan have his head, never dreaming that Mrs Forsyth would be implicated in any way. I would also point out that Officer John Smith went before me this morning, and he stated that not only he, but many other officers dread going to your quarters, as often sweets and other prohibited articles were continually being found on men who had been at work there."

The Doctor was allowed to reply to this statement, and judging by the tone of the reply, he was quite angry. Maybe it was written immediately after he had had a few words with his wife.

"I am very sorry that this has occurred. I accept full responsibility for it, but in doing so I cannot allow Officer John Smith's statement to remain unchallenged. If the officers dreaded going to my quarters as he alleges, it is strange that they remain silent about it, and made no attempts to say something about it. A protest to Mrs Forsyth would have been quite sufficient. Officer John Smith did not make his protest, until after he had been discovered by you. You have my assurance, that this will not occur again, and I should be glad if you would cancel the report."

By now, having read the report thus far, I find it very intriguing as it seems to me that all concerned are trying to cover their backs over a matter that is a little bit delicate. The Doctor's wife would appear to be culpable, for without her involvement the incident could not have happened. Officer John Smith was accused by the Doctor of only reporting the incident after he had been caught red-handed. Was he aware, therefore, that this behaviour was in fact a common occurrence; indeed, did he occasionally sneak a sly cup of tea from Mrs Forsyth himself? Also, why did the Governor instruct John Smith to let 577 Donovan have his head or, in other words, allow him to break some rule and land himself in trouble? What happened to the inmate? Was he also adjudicated upon? This saga is certainly worthy of an hour's viewing as a story on one of television's top soap programmes, if nothing else, as it seems to be full of false allegations, deceit, back-stabbing and, dare I suggest it, a clandestine love affair between the Doctor's wife and the inmate. Fair enough, I will admit to some inventive thinking for that last bit, but then I was told that sex sells more books!

To end this incident the Governor read through all of the evidence, and in my opinion came to the only possible conclusion. He wrote:

"No action taken. This incident was evidently due to the actions of the Medical Officer's wife."

Therefore, Officer John Smith was allowed to resume his normal duties, having probably been suspended from them during the course of the enquiry, and hopefully he steered well clear of 'The Elms' from that time onwards.

Although there are very few written reports against the staff, there are times when the staff need to be disciplined, sometimes even sacked for serious infringements of the Prison's rules. The Governor's Report of November 1949 states very clearly his thoughts on this somewhat delicate matter. He writes:

"Generally speaking the standards of efficiency is good and the staff exercise just that blend of tactfulness and firmness that is so necessary in an establishment of this kind. As I indicated in my previous report, my concern over the amount of trafficking taking place in this prison, and the conviction in November last, and the subsequent dismissal of four members of the staff, for this and other offences, not only confirms my suspicions, but at the same time, has served to rid the service, and especially this establishment, of officers whose actions had an undermining influence, on the general tone and good order of the prison, and added to the difficulties of those responsible for its administration."

Strong words indeed. I would stress that the trafficking taking place in those days was generally of tobacco and nothing of the kind to do with what that term might imply in the present day. This misdemeanour was actually very difficult to prove against an officer, because, generally, the officer smoked himself and the tobacco he carried would have been claimed as being for his personal consumption.

To the question, "Who guards the guards?" the answer is, of course, "The guards!".

CHAPTER EIGHT

The Next Three Decades

IN THE 1950s Parkhurst was still a Preventive Detention Centre, but with a much more relaxed regime. So relaxed, in fact, that an outside visiting football team was allowed into the establishment for the first time, to play against the inmates. Regrettably, history does not record the match score but it must have been a well-contested game as we recently met one of the visiting players who promptly rolled up his trouser leg to proudly show us the scars he had received as a souvenir of that match!

In 1963 work began on the Special Security Block (SSB). Very simply, this building can best be described as a prison within a prison. Leicester and Durham prisons also housed an SSB each. The SSB at Parkhurst was completely self-contained. The reason for this was to provide exceptionally secure accommodation for inmates who had been convicted of committing crimes of particular notoriety. Just after it opened, the majority of the members of the Great Train Robbery gang found themselves starting their thirty-year sentences there. The unit continued to function until Friday, 11th February 1994, when it was suddenly closed, officially for refurbishment. The remaining prisoners, of whom there were six, were 'ghosted' out in the early morning, five sent to the other, still functional SSBs, while the sixth prisoner was down-classified and retained on normal location within Parkhurst. The unit never again opened as an SSB. It was completely re-furbished but when re-opened, nearly four years later, it was as a specialist unit for Protected Witnesses ('super-grasses').

In 1965 the Home Secretary asked the Earl Mountbatten of Burma to write a report of the Inquiry into Prison Escapes and Security. This followed at least five high profile escapes from imprisonment. They included the spy George Blake, who escaped from Wormwood Scrubs in October 1966, and the train robbers, Charlie Wilson and Ronnie Biggs, who broke out from separate establishments within twelve months of each other. Without doubt the greatest embarrassment to the government of the day was the mass escape of nine prisoners who overpowered the driver and guards of a luxury coach that was transporting a total of thirteen prisoners between Winchester and Parkhurst Prisons.

The report was published in December 1966. As might have been expected, it recommended vast changes in the prison service, primarily to tighten up security and prevent further escapes. For Parkhurst, in particular, it recommended that 'multi-handling' dogs should be introduced to patrol the grounds for security purposes. The report reasoned that there were exceptional difficulties in trying to secure the modern inmate within a Victorian establishment, which had not been designed to house the category of prisoners it now held. As recommended, dogs were introduced to assist with the daily running of the prison. They were trained in a variety of roles that included explosives, weapons and drug detection as well as general guard duties.

Earl Mountbatten's main recommendation was that all long-term prisoners, who posed a particular threat to the public, should be held in a single top security prison that would be built specifically for that purpose. Throughout the report various islands, some as far away as the Calf of Man, Muck Island, and Muckle Skerry, and all totally uninhabited, were all considered as the ideal location but each was rejected on logistical grounds. Mountbatten himself favoured using the area alongside Parkhurst,

The Isle of Wight Band photographed outside the Main Gate of Parkhurst some time during the 1920s.

68

Albany, and Camphill prisons as the site for this new establishment which would have held upwards of eighty prisoners. Everything was carefully discussed in the report, including the numbers of staff needed and the additional allowances for working with the country's most dangerous and violent prisoners. As Governor of the Isle of Wight, Mountbatten even suggested the name 'Vectis' for this new, top-security institution. His proposals were, however, eventually rejected in favour of the 'Dispersal System' that was introduced two years later.

This system, which is still in operation today, disperses the most dangerous and violent inmates to specially nominated prisons. The principle behind this is to spread disruptive prisoners around the country, so that at any one time, no single prison would be overloaded with too many difficult or disorderly elements.

No system is perfect and, not surprisingly, most have flaws of one sort or another. Despite the intended aims of the 'Dispersal System', during 1967 and more sinisterly later, in 1969, Parkhurst became overloaded with a large number of very discontented prisoners. Ultimately, the mass unrest, which slowly manifest itself, culminated in a riot. Prior to the major and very serious incident that resulted, a letter, called a 'Round-Robin', signed by 120 inmates, was smuggled out of the prison. The letter stated that certain members of the staff routinely subjected prisoners to brutal treatment. The matter was investigated fully by the appropriate authorities and, subsequently, the Home Secretary of the time, Mr James Callaghan, issued a Press Notice stating that "Parkhurst contained more than the usual number of difficult prisoners with records of violence. The staff had been successful, without going beyond their proper powers, in keeping control in circumstances of inherent tension". Surprisingly, the Governor, Mr Alistair Miller, was never allowed to see the official report into this matter prior to its publication.

Immediately after the report was published, 42 of the 120 signatories to the letter of complaint removed their names from the petition. Obviously this did not go down well with the prisoners in general, as they felt that their petition had not been answered properly. This left a legacy of disquiet and festering

Some of the original buildings at Parkhurst. This picture was taken in 1975.

resentment, such that the atmosphere within the prison remained very volatile.

With the feeling of unrest that was now evident, the staff knew that it would take only the smallest incident to spark off a major problem. An unfortunate development at this point concerned a former Parkhurst prisoner, the Russian spy Peter Kroger, who had been sentenced to 20 years imprisonment for spying. Whilst continuing to serve his sentence at another establishment, the Home Secretary agreed to release him from custody and have him repatriated to Poland. Those inmates who were on 'association', watching Kroger's release on television, became incensed that this traitor had been given two thirds remission off his sentence, whereas all they could expect was one third, if they were lucky. At 6.55 p.m. the same day, at a given signal, between 35 and 40 prisoners pounced on the five officers on duty, making them stand facing a wall, under the threat of being beaten with sticks of broken furniture. At the same time, the billiard table, chairs and other furniture were used to barricade the door, while sharp edged metal meal-trays were handed out to the rioters for use as crude but effective weapons.

Eventually, other officers managed to break down the doors and scramble across the barricades and into the room. As they jumped into the milling crowd of inmates, the men wielding the metal trays cut them down. Many of these prisoners were serving life and, thus, had nothing to lose by their actions. They hurled billiard balls and darts at the approaching officers and smashed windows to arm themselves with broken glass.

By this time all the emergency services on the Island had been put on full alert and every available policeman, prison officer, and doctor was directed to the jail. An area was specially earmarked, away from the source of the trouble, and staffed in readiness by the hospital officers and the Medical Officer. They were kept busy too, for 28 inmates and 35 officers were injured in the fracas. Three prison officers were seriously injured – one had his throat so badly cut that he needed 26 stitches to close the wound. Another had his arm broken and the third suffered a fractured skull.

It is only fair to say that not all the prisoners in the association area that night were involved in the riot, although they would have all known a disturbance was planned. Most of the non-participants were present, either because they were under some form of threat from the other prisoners, or they were just caught up in the speed of the incident, or simply because they did not want to lose face with the rioters. One prisoner in particular, at great personal risk to himself, placed himself between the rioters and the staff who were held hostage, pleading with his fellow inmates not to hurt the officers. To a degree he was successful but remained in fear for his life for some months after. Following the riot, the officers demanded that conveniently placed weapons such as snooker balls and darts should be withdrawn. This must have fallen on deaf ears, because I still today issue these items on a regular basis.

As soon as all the prisoners had been accounted for, most of the staff were stood down and sent home. Those that stayed on duty were amazed when, despite what had transpired, they were ordered to serve the suppertime cup of tea to the inmates. The officers protested, but the senior officer in charge said that the inmates were entitled to their tea, therefore they would get it. The officers, some still sore from the fighting, reluctantly carried out

The old Reception building, on the left, with 'B' Wing and the Segregation Unit beyond. The building at the far end is the old Special Security Unit. The prison's Laundry is on the right-hand side.

the order, to be met by sneers and laughter from the inmates. It was only with the timely arrival of the prison Governor, Mr Alistair Miller, and his quick assessment of the situation that these absurd proceedings were brought to an immediate stop, much to the relief of the officers concerned.

This riot had been started by a hard core of long-term inmates who had planned it as a violent demonstration, simply to make demands on the authorities. Some of the ringleaders were long-term, category 'A' prisoners, protesting against the regime in which they were held almost for the sake of it. They later admitted that they had intended to take over the delicate running of the prison in order to gain the publicity that the 'Round-Robin' had failed to attract.

These prisoners may have failed in their quest for publicity but the riot itself encouraged a vast amount of media attention, as did the subsequent trial that took place at Newport Special Assizes Court in 1970. The trial cost in excess of £150,000, a huge amount of taxpayers' money and with such a high profile trial taking place on the Island, extra Prison Officers and Police had to be drafted in from the mainland to assist in the proceedings, a further burden on the public purse.

Eyewitnesses at the time said it was a spectacle that had never been seen in Newport before. Let us hope that it will never be seen again.

HMP PARKHURST

Under the Prison Act 1952 it is an offence for any person

I. to help a prisoner to escape or attempt to escape; the maximum penalty is 5yrs. imprisonment (section 39 as amended by the Criminal Justice Act 1961);

II. without authority to convey or attempt to convey into a prison or to a prisoner intoxicating liquor or tobacco; the maximum penalty is 6mths. imprisonment or a £50 fine or both (section 40);

III. without authority to convey or attempt to convey into or out of a prison or to a prisoner any letter or other article or to place it outside the prison intending it to come into a prisoner's possession; the maximum penalty is a £50 fine (section 41).

The Prison Act of 1952 as displayed outside the prison's Main Gate.

73

Every form of escape has been tried at Parkhurst, from digging tunnels and 'Trojan-horse' type getaways aboard visiting vehicles to simply going over the wall. It is said that in one incident, an escapee, after having made it beyond the prison's boundary, attempted to get off the Island by boat despite his lack of knowledge of the treacherous tides and currents of the Solent. He was found desperately clinging to a buoy, numb with cold, after his stolen dinghy capsized and sank.

The majority of escape bids are foiled, however, as the Parkhurst Heritage Group's archives reveal. These pictures and accounts illustrate some of the more recent attempts, taken from the many that are recorded in the annals of Parkhurst.

The rear of 'A' Wing, showing the classic knotted sheet. This escape attempt was made on 24th February 1978.

The improvised rope, hanging from a hole where bricks have been removed not from above the cell window, as it would appear, but from below the floor of the cell on the next level up.

A Very Good Attempt

In 1936 one of the most humorous escape attempts took place at Parkhurst. A certain prisoner, who we shall refer to as Johnson, was on the one of the outside working parties, and on this particular day he was assigned to paint the railings at the back of the Governor's house. On this very hot day, the officer in charge quickly became tired, and had a lapse of concentration. Prisoner Johnson, who was a small man with exceedingly large feet, stole this opportunity, and knowing that the Governor was away on holiday, broke the rear kitchen window and entered the house.

Inside he roamed around freely, and eventually came upon the master bedroom. Here, he opened one of the large wardrobes, and discovered to his delight that it was full of ladies' clothing. He then decided on a very spur-of-the-moment escape, and proceeded to dress up in all of Mrs Governor's personal attire. Wearing the latest fashions, including, it is recorded, some very fine underwear, he boldly walked out of the front door, passed the supervising officer, and he headed off in the direction of Newport. Keeping his face hidden behind a large summer hat, he nearly pulled off the cheekiest escape ever. However, as he crossed the cricket pitch, an officer spotted the rather large, size twelve, prison issued boots, under the hemline of the skirt. Realising that an escape attempt was in progress, the officer blew the alarm on his whistle, which forced the prisoner to hoist up his skirts and run for it.

It was, however, a futile attempt, and he was quickly caught. With an officer on each arm, and one behind him, he was frogged-marched back through the prison to the segregation block, all the time, apparently, making his captors laugh with remarks like, "Fancy treating an honest working girl in this fashion, you, you, you ... beasts!".

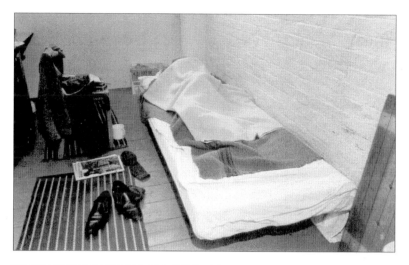

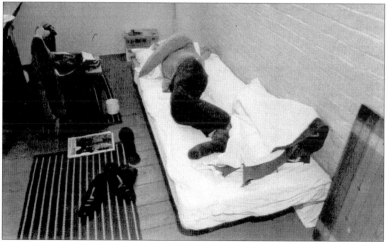

Another audacious escape ruse. In this case the prisoner had hidden in the Wing, having placed a life-size dummy in his bed to fool the officer making the nightly head count. It is not recorded whether the escape attempt succeeded. Note the wooden floor-boards that have since been replaced by concrete.

Funniest Escape Attempt Ever?

This article was printed in a national newspaper around 1938; some of the original has been changed to remove certain words that, now-a-days, are not Politically Correct.

One of the most interesting prisoners we had in Parkhurst was a little fellow, who originated from the West Indies. One day he made up his mind to escape.

It was almost impossible for an ordinary convict to get clear of the Island, so this fellow's chance was a lot slimmer. He managed to secrete on his body a long length of tarred rope that he had stolen earlier. As his outside party returned to the prison for dinner, he managed to break away in the prison yard without being seen.

He tied one end of the rope to a brick, which he threw towards the top of the twenty-foot wall. It missed its mark and fell clattering back into the yard.

Facing the wall, and about twenty yards away, was a big block of cells, and the noise that the escapee was making attracted the attention of all the convicts in their cells. After a few minutes he had a very enthusiastic audience, and they loudly urged him on to renew his attempt.

"Is the screw a commin?" he called out.

"No!" they shouted back

"Dats good", and he threw the brick to the top of the wall, where again it fell short and rattled to the ground. Again he asked if the screw was coming, and again the answer was no, and for the third time he threw the brick and for the third time the brick rattled to the ground.

This sequence carried on for a good many minutes, when, as he was picking up the brick for the eleventh time, a patrolling warder came around the comer and frog-marched him to the Segregation Block.

CHAPTER NINE

The Seventies and Eighties

O NE OF the earliest remaining buildings in the prison is 'C' Wing, which was originally built by the juvenile inmates. In 1970 this accommodation block was set up to house prisoners showing gross personality and behaviour disorders. They were some of the most disruptive convicts in the system and, until this Wing was opened, these men had nowhere to go to receive the proper treatment they needed. The Wing was allocated its own psychologist, its own Governor – Tony Pearson, a Medical Officer – Dr David Cooper, twenty-eight discipline staff and six hospital officers.

All the staff were volunteers and there was no problem in getting the right people to come forward. Considering that nothing like this had ever been attempted anywhere in the world before, the response was remarkable. The majority of the prisoners selected for the unit had short emotional fuses, associated with psychopathic disorders and other behavioural problems.

It was felt that these inmates could benefit greatly by being taken out of the mainstream system and put somewhere where they could be managed by special staff in an entirely different concept. The unit was deliberately kept small, no more than thirty-five inmates, so that they could be monitored properly and, more importantly, so that the stress factors prevalent in the confrontations between staff and inmates might be removed or reduced. As it transpired, this regime did work, as subsequently reported in many publications throughout the world. However, not everyone shared this view.

An article published in the *Sunday Times* claimed that the prison authorities were turning a blind eye to the excessive use of very strong medication to keep unruly and disruptive prisoners suppressed. The article referred to statements made by a former medical officer at Parkhurst who, in another article, published elsewhere, had written that powerful drugs were being administered simply to control difficult prisoners in high security jails. Known colloquially as 'liquid cosh', the drug Depixol was indeed widely prescribed for this category of prisoner but the Home Office denied that it was being used to the extent claimed by the former medical officer.

One lucky prisoner serving at Parkhurst during the 'seventies had a good stroke of fortune, when, on 30th September 1974, he received a Royal Pardon. The pardon document, concerning a man who will be referred to by his initials, D.B.B. (a copy is held by the Heritage Group), was sent for the attention of the Governor. According to the document, D.B.B. had been sentenced to one year's imprisonment for handling stolen property, and another year for taking a motor vehicle without consent and for assaulting a police officer. The jargon says:

"Now know ye that we in consideration of some circumstances humbly represented unto us, are Graciously pleased to extend Our Grace and Mercy unto the said D.B.B., and to pardon and remit unto him forty-two days of the sentences imposed upon him as aforesaid; Our Will and pleasure therefore is that you discharge him out of custody accordingly, and for so doing this shall be sufficient Warrant, By Her Majesty's Command."

A right royal result!

Rear view of 'B', 'A' and 'D' Wings with the Stage Rooms or Association Rooms from where the famous Parkhurst riot of 1969 started.

It was in March of 1979 when a very small minority of IRA prisoners managed to gain access to the roof of 'D' Wing. It was a well-planned protest as they took with them enough blankets and food to last for several days. Once on the roof the four Irishmen along with one British sympathiser systematically stripped the roof tiles from at least a third of the huge building. The tiles were then thrown at the officers and police who were forming a secure perimeter around the area.

Two banners were unfurled, one protesting about the food and conditions at Parkhurst and drawing attention to a fast that involved around one hundred prisoners taking place at the time of the rooftop protest; the other, a white sheet painted in big red letters, simply said "Smash H Blocks", a reference to the Maze Prison (formerly Long Kesh) in Northern Ireland. This prison was simultaneously involved in a protest by terrorists who had been fouling their cells for some months previously as part of their campaign to obtain political prisoner status.

On the third day of the Parkhurst demonstration, it was decided to train fire hoses on the inmates. As it was March time, it was hoped that a good cold soaking would promptly end the protest for the authorities were concerned at the damage that was being done to the structure of the building. This idea, of using fire hoses to quell a disturbance at Parkhurst, was not new having been used way back in 1863 on the women prisoners. Fortunately for these five inmates, though, senior fire brigade officials ruled that it would be too dangerous to play the powerful hoses onto the demonstrators, as the water would probably sweep them off the roof.

During the course of this incident, all the inmates from 'D' and the adjoining 'A' Wing had to be evacuated, for obvious reasons. At the same time, it was decided to move those disruptive prisoners, mentioned at the beginning of this chapter, to other prisons around the country and to use the thus emptied 'C' Wing for the displaced inmates. It was this sequence of events that brought about the premature end to the specialist function of 'C' Wing.

The rooftop demonstration only lasted for a few days for the prisoners eventually gave themselves up peacefully to the authorities but so bad was the damage to the accommodation block ('A' and 'D' Wings), that it was sealed-up and remained closed for the next fourteen years.

The greatest tragedy arising from this incident was the closure of the special unit in 'C' Wing, forcing the return of those prisoners with psychological problems, through no fault of their own, back into the mainstream system. The unit remained closed until December 1985, six years later, when it was once more restored to its role as the accommodation block for prisoners with personality disorders. It even took a few of the original inmates back under its specialist care.

In the following year, a black prisoner at Parkhurst sued the Prison Service for racial discrimination and successfully won his case. It was the first occasion that a prisoner had sued under the Race Relations Act and, as can be imagined, the case attracted a lot of media interest. The prisoner, a West Indian, claimed that he had been refused jobs in both the laundry and the kitchen because he was black. He had wanted a job working, preferably, in the kitchen, mainly for the food perks but also for the warmth that goes with such a much sought-after job. His applications were repeatedly refused, however, and he found himself employed instead on less agreeable work. He decided that he was not being treated the same as other prisoners simply because he was black – grounds for legal action. His case received the backing of the Commission for Racial Equality whose lawyers discovered documentary evidence which revealed that staff had made discriminatory assumptions about him on the basis of his ethnic origin. The Commission regarded the case as a potential landmark for prisoner's rights.

At first the Government attempted to have the case thrown out, on the grounds that prisoners have no right to sue under the Race Relations Act. It argued that all prison operations were matters of national security and therefore immune from prosecution. However, Mr Justice Smithies, at the Southampton County Court, where the case was heard, disagreed, deciding that, because the Prison Department was involved in supplying a service to the public, they could be sued under the Act. As stated earlier, the prisoner eventually won the case and received compensation of several hundred pounds.

As a result of this affair, Race Monitoring was introduced throughout the Prison Service. The Commission asked initially for monitoring to be performed in a number of sensitive areas, including:

- the numbers of black prisoners held in psychiatric Wings and segregation units
- the allocation of black prisoners to certain Wings and cells
- the opportunities available to black prisoners for employment and education inside the jail
- the categorisation methods used by prison staff in relation to blacks and other ethnic minorities.

At the time of this case, in 1986, the Home Office issued its most recent figures, which showed that, of the 26,083 sentenced male prisoners in the United Kingdom, 3,035 were black. Had these figures reflected the ratio of Britain's black citizens to the population as a whole, then the number should have been only 1,300. These statistics raised concerns about the disproportionately large number of black prisoners being held. The Home Office was clearly sensitive to the growing concern regarding this issue, for over some months previous they had issued a range of instructions on the subject of promoting good race relations in prisons. One in particular, which had been distributed just a month earlier, stressed the importance of race relations for the "public position and reputation of the service".

On a completely different subject, Parkhurst has always had, since the earliest days, some form of hospital where patients could be treated 'in house'. It even boasted a small operating theatre which was used regularly to carry out minor operations. In 1987 it was further enhanced when, after a period of closure, it was completely re-furbished and opened as a theatre of a standard comparable with National Health Service facilities. It was exploited as a national Prison Service resource, which meant that prisoners were sent to Parkhurst from all over the country to undergo quite major operations carried out by some of the top consultants then available.

Unfortunately, the facility was closed down in 1996, and all prisoners now have to be escorted to St Mary's Hospital, about half a mile away, for specialist care and operations. This is a very expensive arrangement, though, in terms of the extra security and man-hours required to escort these inmates. Incidentally, the prisoners are not given any special treatment at the expense of the general public. When public sector amenities are used, prisoners are treated the same as the general public and are not allowed to 'jump' the queue or receive preferential treatment in any other way.

Back in 1938, there had been an amusing incident that involved a 70-year-old prisoner who complained of pain in his stomach area. He was diagnosed as suffering from appendicitis; the theatre was warned and the inmate was wheeled in for his operation. All went well and the operation was a complete success, as duly recorded, but someone added an after-note to the report. It said: "Unfortunately, this patient was badly burned over the buttocks by a hot water bottle accidentally left beneath him on the operating table". In those days, of course, they did not have the rubber bottles we use today. Instead, they had to use the large earthenware bottles. One can just imagine the old lag's comments on waking up to discover blisters upon his posterior! The surgeon who operated that day was named Doctor Stratton. He was later the unfortunate victim of an air raid, killed when his house in Church Litten, Newport, was bombed.

When the great hurricane of 1987 swept across Southern England, millions of pounds of damage was caused and Parkhurst did not escape the ferocity of the weather either. Just inside the compound, by the north fence, a large fibreglass dome was located that was being used as a Gymnasium. Without a doubt it was an ugly building but nonetheless it was useful to the establishment, serving a valuable purpose. On the night of the storm, a huge gust of wind lifted this structure from its mountings and threw it over the wall. It landed about thirty metres away, near to Camp Hill farm, where, on impact, it shattered into thousands of pieces. A temporary Gymnasium had to be set up in a completely unsuitable building, restricting the use of the facility to just twelve prisoners at any time. With the prison population then around 500 inmates, it was always a problem to decide who could go to the Gym and who could not.

The White House, one of the original buildings at Parkhurst, facing the original Main Gate. The Pump House is on the right. The large tree in the foreground was one of two destroyed in the 'Great Storm' of October 1987.

A view looking in the opposite direction. Everything that can be seen in the picture was cleared to permit the construction of the new Gate Lodge which was opened in 1991. At the same time the original Main Gate of the prison was walled across as part of Parkhurst's boundary wall. The large trees that were toppled in the 1987 'hurricane' – two Red Cypress – were presented to the prison by the Australian Government in 1844.

The time spent in the Gymnasium is most important to both the inmates and the staff. For the inmates it is a way of relieving stress and aggression that builds up inside them. The staff appreciate this and encourage the inmates to go regularly. Far better for a man to take his aggression out on the weights than on a member of staff. Thankfully, the inadequate exercise facilities soon received attention when a grant was applied for to pay for a new purpose-built Gymnasium.

It was during the 1980s that Parkhurst received its second royal visitor, thereby undoing Queen Victoria's hundred-year mandate. To set the scene, the staff in 'C' Wing had won an award, called the Butler Trust Award, which was presented to them in recognition of the exceptional effort made in attending to their disruptive prisoners. As this was such a prestigious award, Princess Anne, the Princess Royal, was asked if she would kindly present it. This she readily agreed to and, in October 1988, she arrived at the prison on the occasion of the ceremony. Before her arrival, the prison went into overdrive in preparation for the visit. Much of the route she

The original Main Gate on the eastern side of the prison prior to its removal when the new Gate Lodge was constructed.

was to take received a new coat of tarmac, the buildings were cleaned up, and a special toilet was built especially for the Princess, should she be 'caught short'. However, on the day it did not work out quite as planned. As soon as the Princess had presented the award to the members of 'C' Wing, she went on to inspect the prison. All the dignitaries who were present endeavoured to point her in the direction of the route they had previously planned for her. It seems that the Princess had different ideas and determined to go where she wished to go. In the words of one of my colleagues, she saw Parkhurst 'warts and all'. Eventually, after the tour had ended, she went to the visitor area to meet the staff. Over 400 off-duty officers were on parade and the Princess managed to speak to most of them. Without exception, everyone who met the Royal Visitor that day was impressed with the way she conducted herself. It was widely agreed that it had been a memorable occasion.

Parkhurst must be overdue for another Royal Visit.

ONE OF THE LIGHTER MOMENTS

Up until the mid-seventies one of the duties intensely disliked by the staff was the night duty of patrolling the inside of the fence. This duty was commonly known as the Romeo Patrol, as the call-sign for these duties was Romeo 1, Romeo 2, and so on.

To give some form of shelter, wooden sheds were erected at strategic points along the patrol route and, in very cold weather, a brazier or a gas fire was provided for the patrols to warm up occasionally. Of course, as soon as the Orderly Officer passed-by, most of the patrolling was done in the warmth of the hut.

Generally, this practice was carried out by most of the officers on nights, and as long as the Night Orderly Officer kept away, all was OK. The main problem that the night staff would encounter was the regular early morning visit from the Chief Officer. Now, the Chief was certainly a man to fear, especially if you were caught taking short cuts. To put his appointment in military terms, he was the prison RSM. In saying that, it must be remembered that he was also once a basic officer himself and, without doubt, knew exactly what was going on within his domain.

On one particularly cold and very nasty winter's night, one patrol decided that enough was enough, and they opted to stay in the hut all night and benefit from the heat. Far better, they thought, than patrolling outside, especially as it had started to snow very heavily.

In the morning, and only a few minutes before the Chief was due to visit, these two hardy prison officers decided that it was time to surface and get things ready for his arrival. On opening the hut door they both commented on the depth of the snow, for during the night at least three inches had fallen, turning everywhere a beautiful winter's white. This was the moment that they realised that if they had patrolled during the night, as they should have done, there should have been lots of footprints along the patrol route.

The two officers had no choice but to run at full pelt up and down the fence to make it look like they had done their duty properly. On the arrival of the Chief, both men, red in the face, sweating profusely and definitely out of breath, reported to their superior that all was well. The Chief spotted the irregular footprints and, fully aware of what had happened, spoke to the men.

"Thank you", he said, and he started to run away, before he paused and spoke again. "Do you know, gentlemen? I was fully expecting to find you both in the hut, especially in this terrible weather. I fully appreciate that you patrolled the fence throughout the night and such devotion is above and beyond the normal call of duty and, if I had caught you in the hut, I would not have reprimanded you. In fact, gentlemen, I would have congratulated you on using your common sense."

With that he left, desperately trying to stifle the laugh that nearly gave the game away.

CHAPTER TEN

To the End of the Twentieth Century – Great Escapes

FOR A change, the 1990s came in very quietly for Parkhurst. We were the regional winners of the Prison Gardens Competition. Not very exciting compared with some of the previous prison activities, I agree, but still an important achievement. At that time, we held a 'lifer' in the prison who must even then have been in his late sixties. He was a polite old boy who spent all his working days on the garden that is situated in an area where every visitor passing through the prison could admire his handiwork. The lawns were immaculate, the flowerbeds always had something blooming in them, regardless of the time of year, and the whole area was kept weed free.

In 1990 we entered 'his' garden for the regional finals and against some really strong competition 'he' came first. Our gardener was also runner up in '91 and '93; he was even featured on several gardening programs on television. I can still remember this old chap, pottering about in all weathers, always with good advice for anyone who cared to stop by his 'patch' for a chat. He was eventually transferred to a proper lifer's jail on the mainland, and it has to be said that the gardens nowadays, although neat, are nowhere near as smart as they were a few years back when he tended them.

Unfortunately, we managed to lose one of our inmates in October 1991, in rather strange circumstances. Even today, twice a week, the 'Biffa' wagon comes into the prison and is escorted around the establishment collecting the many black rubbish bags. This vehicle is only permitted to enter once the prison roll is correct, that is when all the prisoners have been counted and are locked away behind their doors. Somehow one of our finest managed to evade this roll call, secreting himself on this rubbish vehicle on which he escaped, after it had left the prison. The lorry was checked at the gate, using large mirrors to search the underside and the prisoner was certainly not on top of the vehicle – so the question is, where did he hide on the lorry to escape detection? He was eventually re-captured three months later in London. He was, of course, asked the burning question but, not surprisingly, the prisoner refused to comment!

Moving on another year, the brand new Gym was opened in March 1992 and what a to-do it caused. The general public were incensed that prisoners could have such modern, well-equipped multi-million pound facilities, whereas a lot of the schools were still using equipment and buildings that were 'way beyond their sell-by date'. To mitigate this concern our Gymnasium was made available for use by some outside groups during quiet periods. On Friday afternoons a mini-bus full of disabled children and young adults would arrive, to be met by some of our inmates who, under supervision, would take charge of these visitors and assist them with their exercise routines. Recently we met a lady who regularly attended the Gym for aerobic lessons. The Gym was also available to the prison staff during their dinner and tea breaks.

Fourteen years after the riot that shut 'A' and 'D' Wings, they were eventually re-opened. The reason why they had remained closed for so long was that, during the face-lift, blue asbestos was discovered in the roof space. The careful removal of the material rather delayed the re-furbishment of the two Wings, preventing their re-commissioning until 1993. Once these Wings were back on line, 'B' Wing was earmarked to be next for modernisation. One of the biggest improvements arising from this programme is that every cell is now fitted with internal sanitation. This ended every officer's worst nightmare of receiving a 'potting' by some disgruntled prisoner who had got out of bed on the wrong side. For those who may be mystified as to the meaning of the phrase 'potting', it is the emptying of the contents of a chamber pot over the officer who had the misfortune of being the one who opened the cell door first in the morning.

The 3rd of January 1995 is a date that will remain forever as one of the greatest consequence in the annals of Parkhurst for it proved to be a turning point in the history of this famous prison. The evening of that day started well, when thirty-one prisoners from 'D' Wing went to the Gymnasium for their routine exercise session. Nothing was out of the ordinary, and the session went

DESCRIPTION OF
PRISONER JUST ESCAPED

From H.M. Prison,_____

Date and Hour of Escape	Name and Alias, Offence, Place of Conviction, and Sentence	Born at	Age	Com-plexion	Hair	Eyes and Eyebrows	Build	Height Ft.	Height In.	Trade	Dress Worn at Time of Escape	Distinctive Marks and Peculiarities, with Residence of Friends

Any persons who apprehend, and deliver up the Prisoner, may receive such reward as the Commissioners or Directors of Prisons may consider their services severally justify——not exceeding **FIVE POUNDS** in the whole.

_____

No. 66   [7179—30-3-39]   *GOVERNOR*

The 'Description of Prisoner Just Escaped' form.

---

well. Unfortunately, the prisoners were mis-counted on their way back to the Wing and three of them managed to secrete themselves in the Gym.

From there, once the coast was clear, they made their way via the back door into the metalwork shop where they collected an improvised ladder, constructed from pieces of scrap metal, and escaped over the outside wall.

That is a description of the escape in the simplest terms and, without making excuses, it must be realised that the prisoners have all the time in the world to plan an escape. Besides which, they are also masters of deception.

The officer who was responsible for the inmates as they left the Gym that day was subjected to constant and deliberate interruption during the course of the head-count, to cause him to make a mistake. The 'ladder' that was used was certainly nothing like the one a window cleaner would use. It was a very simple device that, to the unenlightened eye, was no more than a pile of bits and pieces, lying around the shop. It only became a ladder the moment it was needed, when it was carried across the compound and used to scale the perimeter wall.

Once outside, the three could not have known that they had almost ninety minutes before they would be missed. Incredibly, they simply walked to the end of the road where they phoned for a taxi to take them to Sandown airport, from where they planned to steal an aeroplane and fly to freedom (one of the three – a 'lifer' – possessed a private pilot's licence). As it turned out, the plane they broke into had a flat battery and refused to start, thwarting their plans somewhat and compelling them to go to ground, which they did in the Ryde area.

Seven days later they were spotted, ironically, by an officer from their very Wing and the police were quickly informed of their whereabouts. Two of the men were captured immediately and without a struggle but the third decided to make a run for it, only to be captured while trying to cross the River Medina near Whippingham. This escape again attracted worldwide media interest, partly because it was the second escape from a maximum-security prison in less than a year but also because of the extremely dangerous character of the three escapees – two were Category 'A'

Parkhurst hit the headlines with the escape of three dangerous prisoners in the mid-1990s. This was the front page of the Isle of Wight County Press *of 6 January 1995.*

(IoW County Press)

93

prisoners, the third was a 'lifer'! The other escape at that time was from Whitemoor Prison in Cambridgeshire, a purpose-built Category 'A' establishment, which 'lost' a number of armed IRA inmates from their special unit.

As a result of the escape of the three Parkhurst inmates, six members of staff were immediately moved to other prisons. Simultaneously, the Governor, Mr Marriott, was transferred to a headquarters post.

Without going too far into the politics of the situation, it was felt by many staff that Parkhurst was made the scapegoat for both of these escapes. It therefore came as no surprise when the Government-ordered Learmont Report into Prison Security and

---

Parkhurst escape 'bid to embarrass minister'

A DARING breakout from Parkhurst Prison by frequent and careful observation of the genuine key.

Another headline reveals that the escape bid was intended to deliberately embarrass Home Secretary Michael Howard.

(IoW County Press)

Jail downgrading confirmed but staff unsure where axe will fall

ARKHURST is to be
wngraded to a Category B
aining prison with the ex-
cted loss of between 100

Home Secretary Mr Michael Howard.
Although a delegation from the Island led by MP Mr Barry

he was not surprised at the news.
"But I am amazed at the good and positive morale of all

"The security improvemer will be used to very good effe for the Category B prisoner such as the new perimeter fenc

---

Jail downgrading blow to Island

RKHURST Prison is to be stripped
its high security category leading to
likely loss of more than 150 jobs
ich would cause a devastating blow to

a picture of rampant drug abuse and intimida-
tion, with some landings at Parkhurst becoming no go areas for staff.
The jail, which houses some of the most

describes as the unsuitability of Parkhurst for
housing some of the most difficult prisoners in
the system.
The prison service failed to provide technol-

security could be compromised.
In a reference to former governor
Marriott, Mr Howard said he was go
with this recommendation because n

2 0 OCT 1995

Less than a year later, the news breaks that Parkhurst is to be downgraded to a Category 'B' training establishment as recommended in the Learmont Report.

(IoW County Press)

94

the Parkhurst escapes recommended that the prison should be downgraded to a Category 'B' Training Prison. Like Whitemoor, it had been a Category 'A' establishment until then. Obviously, this meant that many discipline staff jobs would be lost. In fact, the final figure was ninety-six, a serious blow to Parkhurst and the local community. Most of these jobs went by natural wastage, early retirement or postings to other establishments, but not all and the effect of such a cut was still keenly felt nevertheless. The uncertainty as to who would or would not go lasted for almost eighteen months, putting extra stress on the staff, who were already under considerable pressure, adapting the prison to a training establishment.

On a completely different subject, the month following the escape saw the opening of the refurbished 'B' and 'G' Wings, leaving 'C' Wing as the only one of the original prison buildings to be modernised. This work was completed by late 1997, when it re-opened as the prison's largest Wing, with 133 cells. At the same time, the decision was taken to downgrade the hospital from a national resource to a facility for the use of only the three Island prisons. A year later and one Wing of the hospital was opened as a detoxification unit, available to prisoners who wished to address their drug problems.

The drug rehabilitation course, which lasts for twelve weeks, has proved to be quite successful, even to the point of one prisoner, who had been an habitual user, helping out on subsequent courses. The Detoxification Programme is important, for drug-related crimes are on the increase. Drug awareness courses, that are also offered, are equally well attended, although most of the students seem to know more about the subject than the staff!

For the remainder of this decade, bringing Parkhurst's history in the 20th century right up-to-date, there is very little to report. Parkhurst is once again going through a quiet spell. We do have the occasional 'ripple' in our smooth exterior, but not enough to ruffle the feathers of the media. The establishment has adopted the 'Progressive Regime' style of man-management for the inmates, which was referred to earlier. In simple terms it is a system of incentives for good behaviour.

On reception, the prisoners go initially to the Basic Wing. From there, to progress through the system, they have to conform to the regime and abide by the compact that they have signed. If they do, then, after a few months, they will move up to the next Wing where they will earn a few more privileges, and, if they continue to conform, they can move up again and so on. All being well, they should pass through the Standard Wings and eventually move onto the Enhanced Wing. Here the extra privileges are many, including more time out of the cell, cooking facilities, more Gym time, and above all, and one of the most important attractions to the majority of the inmates, an in-cell television. This new concession on the Wing is not a 'freebie' – each individual prisoner has to pay for his television out of his weekly wages. At any time, should an inmate misbehave, he will be sent back down to another wing as a punishment. However, if he so wishes, he can keep his head down and once more move back up through the system. Some of the prisoners are quite happy to remain on the Basic Wing, which is fine. There is never any pressure applied by the staff on the prisoners to get them to move up through the system.

As we commence the new millennium, if we stand and look at the old Victorian buildings that still constitute the bulk of Parkhurst's infrastructure, it is very easy to mentally drift back in time and imagine the young juveniles singing 'God Save The Queen', or see the women prisoners rioting in the yard. One can not only conjure up the faces of the heroic convicts who died for their country in World War One, who have only recently been honoured for their gallantry, but also visualise the pure savagery of those inmates who so violently turned on the staff during the riots of 1969.

There have been some very serious times during the prison's history, mirrored by as many absolutely hilarious moments. To save the embarrassment of the inmates and the staff, some of these stories are, perhaps, best left untold or maybe kept for a later, lighter look at prison life. For now, this fascinating story has to end. Most of the tales have been told but, if we recognise Parkhurst for the grand old lady she really is and accord her the dignity properly reserved for senior citizens, we should not anyway reveal her full story but leave her with some of her private memories.

A competition photograph taken by former Governor John Marriott. The original caption was 'Abandon hope, all ye who enter here'.

VOYAGE OF THE 'SIMON TAYLOR'
– THE AUSTRALIAN CONNECTION

THE WESTERN Australian Genealogical Society has a special interest in Parkhurst Prison, through its Convict Historical and Research Group, because the transported boys invariably, at the end of their sentences, settled in Australia, married and raised families. The Society has kindly donated to the Parkhurst Heritage Group a complimentary set of microfiche index to the Parkhurst Prison Registers 1839-1864.

The following passages are extracted courtesy of Jenny Brandis, one of the Society's members, from her web site [http://www.benet.net.au/~brandis/]. They describe one of the typical transportation voyages to Fremantle by the *Simon Taylor* in 1842, and its outcome.

The Success, *one of numerous ships like the* Simon Taylor, *that carried convicts to Australia. Built in 1790, she was still in service 140 years later.*

"The *Simon Taylor* departed from London on 29 April 1842. On board were a total of 245 persons, comprising:

141 adults (82 males and 59 females)
34 children aged between 7 and 14 years (20 males and
    14 females)
44 children aged under 7 years (20 males and 24 females)
26 crew

Included amongst the passengers of the *Simon Taylor* were 18 Parkhurst boys. These boys varied in age from 13 to 16 years and they were being removed from the Parkhurst Prison under a conditional pardon from the Crown (this pardon was forwarded to the Governor of the Colony by the same vessel).

The boys were to be regarded as ordinary emigrants but were subject to the guardian appointed for the voyage, a Samuel Caporn, who was also their teacher for the duration.

The names of the 18 boys were:

Henry BOLTON	Charles DIXON	George DOUGHTY
J. HAREWOOD	Samuel HASLER	S. HOGAN
John Edward LANE	James MORTIMER	Jeremiah MURPHY
J. MURRELL	James NEALE	James NIMMO
John NORTON	Robert STRICKLAND	Samuel TAYLOR
Henry Alexander TOWTON		John TYNE
	Henry WILSON	

During the 111 days non-stop voyage there were two deaths, a male and a female child, both under the age of 7 years. There were also two births – one male and one female.

The *Simon Taylor* docked in Fremantle on Saturday, 20 August 1842. A notice was then inserted in the *Government Gazette* dated 23 September 1842 calling for 'Applicants for the services of any of these boys must be made to John Schoals Esq., Guardian under the Act'.

By the end of 1842, nine boys were in trade, six were farm lads and three were servants."

FURTHER READING: *The Fate of the Artful Dodger* by Paul Buddee is an excellent book on the Parkhurst boys.

APPENDIX TWO

THE STORY OF JOHN GAVIN

JOHN GAVIN was a young teenager who originally started his sentence at Parkhurst and was subsequently transported to Western Australia. Here he murdered his master's son by striking him over the head with an adze (*a cutting instrument similar to an axe*).

There follows an account of the crime taken verbatim from two contemporary Australian publications, *The Inquirer* and *The Perth Gazette*. The first part contains a detailed account of the deed and the trial. This is followed by the account of the execution:

"JOHN GAVIN OR THE ONE THAT FAILED US"

An article published in *The Inquirer*, an Australian newspaper, dated Wednesday, April 10, 1844:

"The General Quarter Sessions of the Peace for the colony was held on Wednesday last before W. H. Mackie, Esq., Chairman, and a full Bench of Magistrates. The calendar only contained four cases, but of these one was for wilful murder, and another for manslaughter.

John Gavin, one of the lads recently sent out from the Parkhurst establishment, was indicted for the wilful murder of George Pollard, the son of a highly respectable settler on the Murray, to whom he was apprenticed, by striking him with an adze. The prisoner was defended by R. W. Nash, Esq., assisted by J. Schoales, Esq., Guardian of a certain class of juvenile Emigrants to which the prisoner belonged, and, being placed at the bar, pleaded not guilty.

The Advocate-General stated the case for the prosecution, which rested entirely on circumstantial evidence.

Jane Pollard, mother of the deceased, being sworn, deposed as follows: I remember Ash Wednesday, 21st Feb last. About the middle of the day between 12 and 1 o'clock, the prisoner came in to dinner, and my son, the deceased, sent him for a gimlet from the carpenter's shop. I recollect then telling my son that I felt very unwell and could not sit up, and I told the prisoner to get up to dinner. I felt as if there was something very heavy over my heart. The deceased recommended I go to bed, and after the prisoner and the deceased sat down to dinner I did go to bed. There was no other person in the

101

house at this time. When I went to my bedroom, I left the prisoner and the deceased in the kitchen. I fell asleep and was awakened by the prisoner coming into my bedroom, with a piece of board in his hand. He said the deceased had sent him to me with the piece of board, which had been broken off a door. There is no door onto my bedroom, nor to my son's. I told him to leave the board there until his Master came home. He had been checked twice that day for slamming a door behind him. The prisoner was not a minute in my room. I then tried to sleep again, but was disturbed by the deceased beginning to sing; he was then in his room, a lean-to next to my bedroom, and the partition wall had not been filled. So that I could hear partly what he said, but not all. The last words I heard him sing were:

> 'And when we close those gates again,
> We will all be true blue.'

The sound of singing then suddenly ceased. I lay a little longer, but I was aroused by some feeling I could not account for, and I leapt out of bed. I exclaimed 'Good God, is there no peace for my afflicted heart', and that I could find no relief but in prayer. I went to the door of my room leading to the kitchen, and as I passed through the doorway I saw the prisoner in the act of drinking out of a basin. He laid the basin on a shelf, and was leaving the kitchen, when I asked him what he was doing. He said he was filling a barrow with straw; he was lifting the straw up in a lazy manner, dropping almost as much as he raised. I asked him if he did not mean to fasten the straw down, and he said that he will do with string. I went into the kitchen to prepare my dinner, and when doing so, the prisoner came in and stooped below the dresser, but did not take or ask for anything. I asked him what had become of the jug of milk, and as he raised himself up I noticed that his lips were very white, and I thought he had been drinking the cream. He went out of the kitchen and I carried on with the preparation of my dinner, and was making some batter when I thought of going to see what the deceased was doing as I had not heard the sound of his flail at the barn. I left the kitchen in the direction of the deceased's door, when I saw the prisoner rush out, of the door looking wild as if in distraction. He began to stoop, and look down and about him, I asked him what he was looking for, he said nothing, I said he could not look for less. He continued walking about in the same way for a minute or so, when I said, 'Why,

Gavin, you are like one losing your senses; are you losing your reason, or what ails you boy?' He made no reply that I heard. He was then walking in the direction of the carpenter's shop. I then went to the door of the deceased's bedroom and saw him lying on his bed, with his back to me. I called him two or three times. I went in and shook him and was surprised at him being so fast asleep in such a short time. There was a coat over and tucked under his head, I removed the coat and saw him in a gore of blood, and thought it might have been from bleeding of the nose. I put my hand under the back of his head. I raised his face a little and he breathed a few times. I clapped my hands and said, 'My child is smothered in his own blood'. I called 'George, my jewel, tell me your murderer'. I am sure that he was not dead when I first raised his head. I called out 'George, George', and 'Johnny Gavin, Johnny Gavin'. My other son Michael came immediately to me and asked what ailed me; I said that Johnny Gavin was after murdering his brother. He asked if he should go immediately and fetch Mr Singleton, I said yes. Michael had been in the barn picking out drake. The Barn may be twenty yards from the house, I cannot recall exactly. My third son Thomas next called to me, I kept going in and out of the deceased's room and saw an adze lying on the floor, and found it covered in hair, and blood, and brains. I found it lying on the floor halfway between the bed and the door. It might have been about a half or a quarter of an hour before Thomas came in. He came up screeching to know what ailed me, and I told him that his brother George had been murdered, and I showed him the bloody adze. He went by my desire to his sister and brother-in-law, who live at a place called Corolayup. Prisoner came next. By that time I suppose my son Thomas had reached Corolayup, which is four miles off by the road, but as I have heard, about two miles through the bush. All the time I kept calling out 'Murder, Murder! Johnny Gavin, Johnny Gavin!'. I saw him come up in a direction from the piggery. When I last saw him, he was going from the house to the carpenter's shop. I said to him, 'Johnny Gavin, Johnny Gavin!', he replied, 'Do you want me madam?' I said, do I want you, where have you been to, or why did you not come to me? When he came up to me and he said that he had been to the river for a drink. When I saw him drinking in the kitchen the bucket was just filled. I said I wondered he was thirsty again so soon after drinking in the kitchen; he said he had not drunk then. Asked him why he had not done so, when he had bought in the bucket for his own use, he said he had forgotten it. I said if you forgot the water, you did not forget to murder my poor child. This passed outside the house. He said he did not and why did I lay it on him, or any other person. I asked who I could lay it on but him, there being no other person on the premises that day but my three children and he. I told him I had seen him coming out of the deceased's room, and had every reason to suspect him. I asked him several times why he did not come to me when I kept screeching for him; he said he did not hear me. He then said, that perhaps a native might have killed the deceased; I replied that there had been no natives there that day, or several days before. He then said maybe he had murdered himself. I said, 'You murdering villain, why should you belie my dead child, he could not take an adze and murder himself on the back of the head'. He then went into the deceased's room and said, George won't say I murdered him; I answered, you did not give him leave to breath. He then called out 'George, George', and I then went to push him away from the bed, he said 'Don't put a drop of blood on me, you said I murdered your child, don't put a drop of blood on me'. I then took notice of his shirt being wet, and said, 'You villain, did you go and wash the blood of my dear child off your clothes'; he said that he had fallen in the river. I do not recollect that I put my hand actually on him, as he stood back and put up his hands to keep me off. I said I would have the shirt off him. I put my apron around my hand and seized him by the shirt collar, and pulled the shirt off him in order to let Mr Singleton see the shirt was wet. I used the apron to prevent the blood on my hands staining his shirt. He wanted another shirt from me, and went with me to the kitchen, and I shut both the front and back doors upon him. I saw a chord lying on a chest, and tied his left hand, which he let me do without resistance, but he struggled much against my tying his right hand, but I got stronger, as he got weaker, and I tied both his hands at last. There were two large rooms in the kitchen, and he began to look about, and I was afraid he would escape, so I took him into the deceased's room, because there was only one door to guard, and only one window too small to escape through. I had a stick in my hand, which I took up to guard him, and, somehow or other he got hold of the stick, and I had a hard struggle to get it back. He said that he would swear against me for making him a prisoner and hurting his hands. After this he came out of the deceased's room, I retreated before him, and he then knelt down before me and said, 'Do forgive madam, and don't say I murdered your son, and I will pray for George', he said so several times. I said that he had not given George time to pray. After that, he said at different times, 'Do madam, blow my brains out'. I said I would not imbrue my hands in his blood, as he had done with my son, and that I would deliver him to the law. After this he became more case hardened, and said he did not regard what I could do, as I did not see him do it. He kept coming up to me, and placing his hands against me, and saying 'I didn't' in an impertinent way. He kept doing this till the soldier Longworth came up to me, followed by another person and Corporal Alcock. I knew that the deceased had borrowed a book of songs. I found the book of songs in the deceased's bed. The next day I looked into the book to find the words I had heard him singing, but could not. Afterwards my daughter found the words in a page glued to another page by blood. I did not see any stains of blood on prisoner's clothes. The adze now produced is the one I found in the deceased's bedroom. The trousers produced are those the prisoner had on the day in question. The adze is my husband's. The handle was not loose as it now is when I found the adze in the deceased's room the handle was then in the iron socket. I lifted it by the handle. The prisoner was an apprentice of my husband's. The river opposite our house was half the depth of a pork barrel in the deepest part. Prisoner had told me that he had fallen in the river at a spot where there were two or three pork barrels in the river, and near the bank. They were so close that a person could not have fallen into the river between them and the bank.

Cross-examined: I did not see anything particular in the conduct of the prisoner and deceased to each other at dinner. I took no notice of their conversation. Deceased did not tell prisoner to go for the gimlet in an angry manner. I never knew of any quarrel between them. I recollect deceased saying to prisoner, come away, and don't stand to be blowed up in this manner. Sometimes I had reproved both prisoner and deceased, but not repeatedly. Whenever I heard him sing any words. The tunes the prisoner hummed were not psalm tunes to my knowledge. Gavin called me twice a little louder than usual, when he bought me in the piece of wood. When the sound of the deceased singing suddenly ceased, I did not hear any other sounds. The uneasiness I felt had nothing to do with the prisoner. I observed that the prisoner's lips looked white, as soon as he came into the kitchen, and before he stooped under the dresser. He must have known then that I was in the kitchen. I did not suppose that he meant to hide himself. He came in quickly and stooped down under the dresser, and was going out as quickly, when I asked him who had drunk the milk, he then turned partly round to me, and then I observed his lips. Deceased was a good deal taller and larger than the prisoner. When I saw the prisoner coming up from the river, he was coming very slowly. I could not tell at first tell whether he was moving or standing. I saw his face was as clean as if just washed, but did not notice if his head was wet. He did not say anything about a dog drinking out of the bucket in the kitchen. I did not observe any marks of blows about the deceased's mouth. I have often heard the deceased singing out of the book produced. I never heard the prisoner express any dislike to any song in the book. I do not know that any one had told the prisoner to carry away straw. There had not been a pig killed about the premises for three weeks before. I do think that fresh bloodstains can be effaced by washing. I remember a dish of blood being in my room from Saturday to a Monday, on a chest. That was from a fortnight to three weeks before Ash Wednesday. The prisoner was not present at my examination before Mr Singleton.

By the Court: From the time I got up out of bed until the time I saw him lifeless, was about five or six minutes. No creature was on the premises that day except myself, the deceased, and my sons Michael and Thomas, and, the prisoner. Thomas is between 10 and 11, and Michael is between 7 and 8. When the prisoner came he said his age was 14. I neither saw nor heard of any natives about the premises that day, except what the prisoner spoke of.

Thomas Pollard: I am a son of the last witness. I recollect the day my brother was killed; I was then out in the bush with the cattle. I heard my mother cry out, Johnny Gavin; I was at a distance since measured of 800 yards from my father's house. I ran up to my mother and asked what was the matter; she said that Johnny Gavin had murdered my brother George. I went into the room to see my brother, but I could not tell whether he was dead or alive. I went off to my brother-in-law's. I run there. As I approached the dwelling house when my mother called out, I saw the prisoner going round the carpenter's shop as if he was going into it. The carpenter's shop

106

is close to the house. He ought to have heard my mother calling out much more plainly than I did.

Cross-examined: I have never heard the prisoner sing or read out of the book produced. I have heard deceased sing songs out of it, in the prisoner's hearing, who did not appear at all annoyed at the songs, but continued with whatever he was about.

F. C. Singleton, Esq: I am the Committing Magistrate, Mrs Pollard gave me in substance, the same account she has told the court today. She told me far more, but I took down only so much as I considered necessary. I was at Pollards the night of the murder and examined the body. It was laying on and across a straw bed, about the height of this court table, in a lean-to. I found the head cleft to pieces, a continuation of wounds, quite a mash of brains, skull and hair. I gave directions for the body to be washed. Early next morning I returned to Pollards, and with Sergeant Burrell examined the body again. I found two wounds on the face, one across the cheek bone and nose, the other across the temple, part of three fingers severed, one cut behind left ear, several blows to the back of the head, smashing the skull into a number of pieces, in a slashing direction, nine inches long. I measured the several distances referred to. I saw no appearance on the banks of the river as if any one had fallen. The river there is only 18 feet wide, 2 feet 3 or 4 inches deep, six feet from the bank. The carpenter's shop is 22 yards from the house. Where Thomas Pollard was herding the cattle when he heard his mother call, was 800 yards from the house. The spot where the prisoner said he fell in was 48 yards from the house, and the spot where he said he came out was 13 yards. During Mrs Pollard's examination the prisoner was kept outside in the custody of two soldiers. Afterwards, and while she was present, I read over her deposition to him, and asked her if it was all right, and she said yes, but I did not re-swear her in his presence. He put questions to her. I saw a pork barrel in the river just opposite the part of the bank at which the prisoner said he had drank. The prisoner was examined by me two or three hours after the deceased was found dead, he was then stripped of his trousers, now produced, which were quite wet, and they were left in the keeping of a soldier. The next morning I examined the trousers, when dry, and discovered what I conceive, spots of blood, which I now point out.

Joseph Harris Esq., acting Colonial Surgeon: I have heard the description given by Mr Singleton of the wounds received by the deceased. I am of the opinion that the wounds are sufficient to cause instant death. I am surprised to hear that deceased breathed at all after them. I think such wounds were likely to be inflicted by such an instrument as the adze produced. I think a boy like the prisoner is capable of inflicting such wounds with such a weapon.

The prisoner, in his statement to the committing magistrate, denied all knowledge of the deed, and accounted for the wet state of his clothes by having fallen in the river; and for the blood upon them by Mrs Pollard touching him when tying his hands. It was also stated that he and the deceased were on very good terms; the deceased always taking the prisoner's part, and on one occasion saved his life while bathing.

A long and able defence was made for the prisoner by Mr. Nash. Council commenced by stating the very high character, in every respect borne by the witness Mrs Pollard, on whose evidence the case mainly rested; but argued that her memory and temper had been much shaken by several previous family afflictions; and that viewing her previous dislike to the boy, and her prejudice against him as a prisoner, it was likely that she would at once satisfy herself that he was the murderer, without stopping to inquire much into the circumstances. The learned gentlemen also entered into an able analysis of Mrs Pollard's evidence, tending to show that all of the actions and expressions of the accused, viewed and stated by a person so prejudice, and whose mind was so fully made up, would be indications of guilt, while viewed in the manner stated by the learned Council they might be taken as evidence of innocence. The total absence of any ill feeling, and of any motive to give probability to the commission of the murder by the prisoner, was put forward in a very strong manner; and the argument was summed up of instances of the danger of relying on circumstantial evidence.

A point was also raised by Council in favour of the prisoner, that it appeared in evidence that he had not been present when the depositions were taken by the committing magistrate; and that consequently he had been wrongly sent to prison; he was therefore illegally here, in fact, in the eyes of the law, he ought not to be considered as being on his trial at all. In support of this point, Council entered into a long and very able argument, the gist of which is as follows: The right to inquire and commit was given; and on a case occurring as to the use of depositions as evidence, reference was made to this statute for essential, and the statute, which applied to all inquiries, was construed to require the presence of the accused. The necessity of this presence having been derived from a statute directing depositions generally, all depositions must be so taken, and if not so taken, were not to be viewed as depositions at all. The committal consequently was illegal, a writ of 'habeas corpus' would have discharged the prisoner, and if so the Court could in like manner direct his discharge when the point was discovered by evidence. Council was not aware that the point had ever been ruled, but that was no reason why it should not be. Formerly, if the objection had been raised in the courts at home, it would have been, most likely, over-ruled, because the practice had been, formerly, very harsh against a prisoner, but it was not so now, there being a strong tendency at home to assimilate to civil cases, as to all points of benefit to the accused. Council contended that technical objections, which would not have been listened to 20 years ago, were now favourably received by the courts at home, that the principle of affording every benefit to accused persons was daily extending. As instances of the increased humanity with which the law acted, he quoted the passing of the Prisoners Counsel Bill, and the reversal of the sentence of the Court in the case of Lovett, so well remembered here. He looked upon that case as another step in justice; it had been so ruled because there had not been the fullest fair play, and every opportunity given. There had to be a defect, all subsequent to it was void.

The court was very decidedly of opinions that the objection was not valid, all the witnesses being present; the depositions might be disposed of altogether.

The chairman having summed up, the jury retired, and having consulted together for about half an hour, returned a verdict of guilty. Sentence of death was passed upon the prisoner, the Court observing that although the conviction was on circumstantial evidence, it was never-the-less of so satisfactory a nature, and the crime itself so utterly wanting in any palliating circumstances, that it could hold out no hope of any remission of the sentence. (It will be seen that the prisoner has since made a full confession of the dreadful crime.)"

Next is an account of the circumstances leading up to the murder of George Pollard, as confessed by the prisoner, John Gavin, and of his subsequent execution, published originally in *The Perth Gazette*, date unknown.

"Confession of the Murder of George Pollard:

To all parties it must be consolatory to know, that on Friday night and Saturday morning, the unfortunate criminal confessed his guilt, and this in so ample and sincere manner as to leave not a doubt on the mind of Mr Schoales, who received that confession, that anything remained behind. The substance of the confession was, that the first thoughts of committing the crime arose in his mind just five minutes before the execution of the deed; that it was a sudden instigation, one which had been paralleled, but not frequently. The boy sat down to dinner with his victim without a thought harboured in his mind of harm towards him. He had made up his mind to murder the mother of the family that afternoon, and as he commenced his work about the farm while the lad Pollard was sleeping, the thought flashed across the mind of the prisoner, that if he murdered the woman first, then a lad stronger than himself remained on the premises, able to take him prisoner, and that to secure the fate of the woman and his own safety, he must first kill the lad. In explanation of the circumstances of his clothes being wet, the unfortunate lad stated that he went to the river, not to drink, nor to wash blood from his clothes, but to drown himself, but that his courage failed him, such was his feeling and remorse at the act he had committed. He could state no possible reason why he compassed the death of Mrs Pollard.

EXECUTION:

The convict was transferred to Freemantle Goal on Thursday afternoon, where he was attended with the utmost attention by the Rev. George King. On Good Friday the reverend gentleman was in prayer with the lad before the hours of service, and again in the afternoon, and to an advanced hour of the evening. On the same evening, Mr Schoales placed himself in communication with the boy, remaining with him during the time the clergyman was affording the consolations of the Church. Extreme penitence, the utmost contrition, and the fullest confession, marked his behaviour. At daylight Mr Schoales was again in attendance, and Mr King attended at an early hour. At 8 o'clock the preparations were complete, which were made with every attention to the proper execution of the sentence; at the same time ensuring the least possible suffering to the unfortunate lad. The prison bell then began to toll, and the melancholy procession set out from the condemned cell to the scaffold. The Sheriff and his deputies and constables, the Rev. G. King, was reading appropriate passages of Scripture, the prisoner, supported by Mr Schoales, and lastly more constables, closed the train.

The boy was deeply affected, and was assisted up the steps to the platform. From this time the proceedings were rapid, and at ten minutes after eight, the cart was moved forward, and the criminal was launched into eternity. So light was the body that, with a humane attention, heavy weights were attached to the legs of the sufferer, a precaution the property of which was evinced in the fact, that apparently the pangs of the unhappy boy were very few. Having hung for an hour, the Sheriff resigned the custody of the body to Mr Schoales, who had it cut down, placed in a decent shell, and removed for the purpose of interment.

The place of execution was about ten yards on the left of the jail, looking towards the church. The assemblage of people was not very great, and proper precautions for decent behaviour on such a solemn occasion were taken and provided for, by the presence of the Constables and a detachment of Her Majesty's 51st Light Infantry who kept the ground. After death, an excellent mask of the face and cast of the skull were taken, for the purpose of furthering the ends of science. The head, we understand is of extraordinary formation; the anterior organs being very deficiently developed, while the posterior organs are of an enormous size.

At 4 o'clock p.m.. the body was committed to the earth in the sand-hills a little to the southwest of the Courthouse, accompanied by Mr Schoales alone, and carried by a fatigue party of prisoners of the jail. There, without rite or ceremony, the remains of this miserable lad were inhumed, but though the place of his Sepulchre is unknown to all, yet may God grant that the awful example made on so a young lad, may ever be before the minds of all of us young or old."

Appendix Three

THE CATEGORY SYSTEM

PRISONERS TODAY, rather than the prisons they are held in, are categorised into four groups: 'A', 'B', 'C' and 'D'.

Category 'A'

These are prisoners who have the potential to escape an establishment with outside help. The escape would cause embarrassment to the authorities and would pose a threat to society.

Category 'B'

These inmates also have the capability to escape with outside help. As for Category 'A' prisoners, they are held in conditions that would make an escape attempt difficult.

Category 'C'

These are prisoners who can be held in semi-open conditions. Should they escape, it would not pose any threat to society.

Category 'D'

These prisoners are held in establishments under open conditions. There are no locks and the prisoners have a great deal of freedom. Inmates of this category are generally at the end of their sentences, the prisons they are held in being used as rehabilitation centres for life on the outside.

HMP PARKHURST – LIST OF GOVERNORS

Capt R. Woolcombe	26.12.1838–30.06.1843
Capt G. Hall	23.08.1843–01.04.1864
Mrs Sarah Wilson	01.03.1864–30.04.1869
Capt W. S. Cockworthy	12.06.1869–06.01.1870
Maj F. H. Noott	15.01.1870–31.08.1887
Capt W. T. Harvey	01.06.1888–07.03.1889
Capt F. Johnson	01.03.1889–22.02.1892
Lt Col B. Partridge	07.03.1892–01.07.1896
Lt Col H. Plummer	02.07.1896–15.11.1900
Capt C. E. De Eardley Wilmot	16.08.1900–29.02.1904
Capt H. L. Conor	01.03.1904–14.08.1910
Capt H. R. Guyon	13.09.1910–24.04.1915
Capt R. H. D'Aeth	27.07.1915–30.06.1926
Lt Col H. M. A. Hales	01.07.1926–31.08.1930
Capt G. F. Clayton	01.09.1930–06.03.1935
Mr M. A. Scott, M.C.	17.04.1935–22.06.1937
Cmdr F. A. P. Foster	27.07.1937–01.02.1940
Capt F. H. L. Stevenson	01.03.1940–30.09.1944
Cmdr A. L. Sanders	01.10.1944–30.06.1945
Capt E. C. Tunnicliffe	01.06.1946–15.05.1947
M. A. Horrix	16.05.1947–14.11.1951
Mr P. A. Marriott	15.11.1951–31.08.1959
Mr S. T. E. P. Ennion	01.09.1959–31.05.1961
Mr A. C. Packham	07.06.1961–03.01.1966
Mr A. Miller, M.B.E., T.D.	31.01.1966–24.08.1970
Mr M. D. MaCleod	28.08.1970–30.10.1973
Mr M. Bryan	30.01.1973–31.10.1977
Mr C. T. Pratt	30.04.1977–30.04.1980
Mr J. R. Sandy	13.05.1980–30.06.1982
Mr A. H. Rayfield	05.07.1982–02.02.1985
Mr J. H. Rumball	04.02.1985–10.01.1986
Mr R. E. Withers	10.03.1986–13.01.1989
Mr J. Blakey	14.01.1989–25.09.1990
Mr J. Marriott	13.10.1990–10.01.1995
Mr D. M. Morrison	16.01.1995

HMP PARKHURST – LIST OF DEPUTY GOVERNORS

G. Shirlaw	01.10.1843–31.08.1862
Capt J. F. Bell	01.10.1872–19.05.1878
Capt G. Kemmis	02.07.1878–05.12.1883
W. H. O. Russell	01.03.1884–16.05.1889
Lt Col F. Lodge	01.10.1889–24.03.1897
Lt Col C. H. B. Farrant	01.04.1897–25.05.1899
Capt The Hon C. T. Holland	24.04.1899–01.09.1901
Capt G. E. Temple	02.09.1901–05.04.1904
Maj G. R. Elliott	01.06.1904–22.04.1907
Maj B. H. Boucher, D.S.O.	07.05.1907–15.11.1911
H. G. Supple	01.11.1911–01.03.1912
Lt R. M. Tabuteam, R.N.	12.12.1912–05.10.1919
A. E. Scott, M.C.	08.08.1919–09.03.1923
Maj C. Pannall, D.S.O., M.C.	23.08.1923–17.04.1928
Comdr A. L. Saunders, R.N.	20.07.1928–02.11.1929
P. A. Marriott	23.11.1929–07.12.1930
S. T. E. P. Ennion	08.12.1930–24.05.1933
Maj B. S. K. G. Guise–Moores, M.C.	09.06.1933–01.09.1937
Comdr S. W. Lushington, R.N.	01.10.1939–19.11.1939
J. R. G. Bantock	20.11.1939–30.01.1942
Flt Lt L. Newcombe	31.01.1942–10.08.1942
J. S. Tenswell	23.03.1945–15.10.1946
Lt Col J. W. A. Parkin	15.10.1946–10.01.1949
Maj G. F. Bride	10.01.1949–05.05.1952
G. E. Griffiths	05.05.1952–03.10.1955
E. A. Esquilant	03.10.1955–27.03.1958
M. S. Winston	25.04.1958–08.09.1958
J. P. Cox	09.12.1958–05.02.1962
R. L. D. Skrine	05.02.1962–13.09.1965
C. B. Heald	13.09.1965–01.09.1969
Lt Comdr S. E. Hawkins	20.10.1969–15.06.1972
D. J. Thompson	15.06.1972–30.08.1976
B. V. Smith	31.08.1976–03.10.1979
D. M. Morrison	29.10.1979–30.04.1985
J. R. Dovell	15.07.1985–11.11.1986
W. A. Wood	16.03.1987–03.02.1991
K. P. P. Rogers	04.02.1991–13.11.1993
R. Walker	01.11.1993–

Parkhurst Prison at night, a photograph taken in 1978, looking to the south.

OTHER BOOKS FROM
COACH HOUSE PUBLICATIONS LTD

THIRTY YEARS HARD LABOUR?
*A classic collection of over fifty stories
from inside some of Britain's toughest jails*
By Dave Pritchard
Illustrated by Chris Timothy

ALUM BAY AND THE NEEDLES
SHIPWRECKS OF THE WIGHT
Both by John C. Medland

WINGS OVER THE ISLAND
The Aviation Heritage of the Isle of Wight
By David L. Williams

PASTORAL PILGRIMAGE
– walks on the Isle of Wight
Written and illustrated by Victor Vivian

GHOSTLY ENCOUNTERS
as experienced by Isle of Wight psychic
Margo Williams

COLOURFUL CHARACTERS OF THE ISLE OF WIGHT
VILLAGE CHURCHES OF THE ISLE OF WIGHT
TRAVELLERS' JOY
– living and walking on the Isle of Wight
"QUEEN MARY": EARLY YEARS
LONG LIVE THE "QUEEN MARY"
All by Ron Winter